# From Out Of Our Christian Treasure

## Other CSS titles by Stan Purdum

- *Sermons on the Gospel Readings, Series I, Cycle A* (with other authors)
- *Sermons on the First Readings, Series II, Cycle B* (with other authors)
- *Worship Resources for Special Sundays* (with other authors)
- *Hear My Voice* (with other authors)
- *Sermons on the First Readings, Series II, Cycle A* (with other authors)
- *New Mercies I See*
- *Playing In Traffic*
- *Sermons on the Gospel Readings (Series II, Cycle B)* (with other authors)
- *Christmas Treasures* (with other authors)
- *Leading to Easter* (with other authors)
- *Sermons on the First Readings, Series II, Cycle C* (with other authors)

# From Out Of Our Christian Treasure

Sermons for the
Season After Pentecost
(First Half) Based on the
Gospel Lessons for Cycle A

Stan Purdum

CSS Publishing Company
Lima, Ohio

FROM OUT OF OUR CHRISTIAN TREASURE

FIRST EDITION
Copyright © 2025 by
CSS Publishing Company, Inc.

Published by CSS Publishing Company, Inc., Lima, Ohio 45807. All rights reserved. No part of this publication may be reproduced in any manner whatsoever without the prior permission of the publisher, except in the case of brief quotations embodied in critical articles and reviews. Inquiries should be addressed to: CSS Publishing Company, Inc., Permissions Department, 5450 N. Dixie Highway, Lima, Ohio 45807.

Scripture quotations marked (NRSV) are from the New Revised Standard Version of the Bible. Copyright 1989 by the Division of Christian Education of the National Council of the Churches of Christ in the USA, Nashville, Thomas Nelson Publishers © 1989. Used by permission. All rights reserved.

**Library of Congress Cataloging-in-Publication Data**
Names: Purdum, Stan, 1945- author
Title: From out of our Christian treasure : sermons for the season after
   Pentecost (first half) based on the gospel lessons for Cycle A / Stan
   Purdum.
Description: First edition. | Lima, Ohio : CSS Publishing Company, [2025]
Identifiers: LCCN 2025032631 (print) | LCCN 2025032632 (ebook) | ISBN
   9780788031397 paperback | ISBN 9780788031427 adobe pdf
Subjects: LCSH: Pentecost season--Sermons | Bible. Gospels--Sermons |
   Common lectionary (1992). Year A | Sermons, American--21st century
Classification: LCC BV4300.5 .P87 2025  (print) | LCC BV4300.5  (ebook)
LC record available at https://lccn.loc.gov/2025032631
LC ebook record available at https://lccn.loc.gov/2025032632

For more information about CSS Publishing Company resources, visit our website at www.csspub.com, email us at csr@csspub.com, or call (800) 241-4056.

e-book:
ISBN-13: 978-0-7880-3142-7
ISBN-10: 0-7880-3142-2

ISBN-13: 978-0-7880-3139-7
ISBN-10: 0-7880-3139-2                          PRINTED IN USA

*To a new generation: Niko, Kaito and Cypher Rose*

# Contents

Introduction .......................................... 9

Trinity Sunday......................... Matthew 28:16-20
Making Disciples ..................................... 11

Proper 5 ......................... Matthew 9:9-13, 18-26
Jesus The Initiator, The Responder, And The Waylaid ...... 18

Proper 6 ....................... Matthew 9:35-10:8 (9-23)
Feeling It In The Gut ................................. 24

Proper 7 ............................. Matthew 10:24-39
Rethinking Your Neighborhood........................ 31

Proper 8 ............................. Matthew 10:40-42
What's The Reward?................................. 38

Proper 9 ....................... Matthew 11:16-19, 25-30
Wear The Light Yoke ................................. 45

Proper 10 .......................... Matthew 13:1-9, 18-23
The Emotional Gateway ............................. 52

Proper 11 ..................... Matthew 13:24-30, 36-43
On Being Long-Tempered ........................... 59

Proper 12 ..................... Matthew 13:31-33, 44-52
Bringing Out Of Our Christian
Treasure What Is New And What Is Old ................ 64

Proper 13 ............................. Matthew 14:13-21
Jesus, And The Wisdom Of Strategic Withdrawal.......... 71

Proper 14 ............................. Matthew 14:22-33
Out At Sea With Simon Peter......................... 77

Proper 15 ..................... Matthew 15:(10-20) 21-28
Faith Is A Verb ........................................ 83

Proper 16 ............................. Matthew 16:13-20
Your Key To The Kingdom ........................... 89

Endnotes ............................................ 97

# Introduction

Preaching is a privilege. In addition to whatever benefit the people in the pews may receive from our sermons, preaching also helps us who deliver homilies to participate in the conversation of life. It gives us a platform from which to offer views that in the best of our preaching, are more than mere opinions or biases and are instead our best efforts to bring a biblical perspective, aligned with a compassionate sense of what it means to be human, to the perplexities of daily living — and to do all that without using the Bible as a club with which to beat hearers into submission to our understandings — and sometimes our *mis*understandings — of the Christian faith.

Preaching is also a privilege because it allows us to preach honestly to ourselves and bring the resources of faith, hope and love to help us be the people we yearn and strive to be — and which we believe God calls us to be. And in doing so, we are sometimes able to help people who hear our words find a way forward in their own struggles with the pain of being human.

The sermons in this volume were driven first by the lectionary, which dictated the texts I should wrestle with, and second by a determination to be honest about their application to *my* life and the lives of those who listen to me when I step into the pulpit.

May God help all of us who preach to use our privilege humbly, thoughtfully, faithfully and compassionately.

Stan Purdum
November 2024

Trinity Sunday
Matthew 28:16-20

# Making Disciples

Several years ago, a woman I knew who was involved in a prison ministry asked me if I would be willing to undertake the "discipling" of an inmate who had come to profess Christianity under the guidance of the ministry group. She said the man — I'll call him Hank — felt he had a lot of spiritual growing to do, and he thought it would be helpful for him to have some personal direction in the Christian faith.

I agreed to do it, and I had my initial contact with Hank through an exchange of letters. Eventually, I went to the prison to visit him, something which I did several times, and over the course of the visits, I learned his story.

He had been arrested on charges of domestic violence and criminal damage after breaking into his girlfriend's house and beating her up. Alcohol had been involved, but it was no excuse. Although he'd originally received a relatively short sentence that he was to serve in a minimum-security unit, he had taken advantage of the low security and walked away from the facility. He was subsequently apprehended by the police, and received an additional sentence for escaping, which he now had to serve in a more secure prison. At the time I met Hank, he'd been incarcerated for nine years.

At our first face-to-face meeting, Hank repeated the request the woman had passed on to me: He wanted me to "disciple" him. It became clear to me that he had learned this term from his attendance at the program the Christian ministry ran inside the prison walls.

We are used to hearing the word "disciple" as a noun to refer to followers of Jesus, and disciple means "learner." But Hank, and the ministry group were using it as a verb, so that disciple not only described what one *was*, but also what one *did* — one learned about the way of Jesus in order to behave in ways that reflect Jesus' example and teaching. In using disciple as a verb, the ministry was not putting a new spin on the word, however; Matthew, the New Testament writer, did the same thing in a few places in his gospel. One of those locations is in today's reading, where Jesus told his eleven disciples (noun usage) to *"make disciples* of all nations."[1] While the English says "make disciples," the original Greek is all one word, and if we were to translate it literally, we'd need to use something like "disciple-ize."

The prison ministry group had it right, for the following of Jesus is a learning process. The group taught inmates how to start on the Christian road — they invited conversions — or to use a different phrase, they "led people to Christ." But the group was right that that was only the first step. For discipleship to blossom, beginners in the faith need instruction.

Jesus himself made the same point in today's reading when he said that in addition to baptizing new converts "in the name of the Father, and of the Son, and of the Holy Spirit" (the vocabulary that makes this passage apropos for Trinity Sunday) the eleven should "[teach] them to obey everything that I have commanded you." New converts need good mentors in Christian living, and they need the fellowship of a Christian community, a congregation. All of that is part of discipling.

When someone disciples another person, the implication is not that the mentor has Christianity all figured out and is a perfect Christian. Rather the mentor, who is him- or herself a disciple of Jesus', is simply further along the Christian journey and has some experience to share with the beginner in the faith.

In practice, discipling Hank was not a straightforward process. At times his willingness to even talk about the Christian life was overwhelmed by his desire to have an advocate to help him be released from prison. I soon recognized that I could be that advocate. There was a case to be made that he had served enough time for his crime, and when a release hearing came up, I spoke on his behalf and told the judge what kinds of support my congregation was willing to provide. In the end, the judge released Hank to a halfway house, where he started rebuilding his life. My church helped to meet some of his needs there, and after he was fully released, I officiated at his wedding when he remarried the woman who had been his wife at the time he took up with the girlfriend.

In time, Hank also joined my church, but he lived too far away to attend often, and my attempts to connect him with a church nearer at hand were unsuccessful. And when I later moved out of state, we lost touch. Sometime after that, I learned that he'd gotten in trouble again in a bad act similar to his earlier offense, with alcohol again being an aggravating factor in his wrongdoing. As of this writing, he is back in prison.

I can't say that Hank received no spiritual benefit from our time together, or even that his latest imprisonment means that he has lost his faith. I simply don't know, and I'm not in a position to judge what's in his heart. Hank has his stumbling blocks and makes some bad decisions. I certainly can't excuse what he has done, but I continue to pray for him.

You'll not be surprised when I say that discipling can be hard work and carries no guarantees that those whom we seek to help on the faith journey won't make any wrong turns.

Nonetheless, although Jesus spoke these words about discipling to his eleven followers who became apostles, the church has never understood Jesus' command here to be an obligation of simply those few. Rather, we call Jesus' command here "The Great Commission," and see it as a call to *all Christians in every age.* Earlier in his gospel, Matthew used the word "disciples" to refer exclusively to the inner group of twelve men who left all to follow Jesus. But now, in today's passage, the remaining eleven became representatives for all Christians in the post-Easter church. After the resurrection, the invitation to discipleship was open to everybody, and the commission to make disciples became the work of all Christians.

But we've said that making disciples is often hard work. We can take some comfort in the fact that we are called to be faithful, but not necessarily effective. That is to say, we are not called to do what only God can do, for we can instruct another person about the faith, but it is God who changes a person's heart. As the apostle Paul wrote the Corinthians, "I planted, Apollos watered, *but God gave the growth*. So, neither the one who plants nor the one who waters is anything, *but only God who gives the growth*" (1 Corinthians 3:6-7, emphasis added). Still, we shouldn't make that an excuse. We do need to be faithful and give discipling our best effort.

We can also take heart in the reality that disciples, whether new ones or existing ones, are not called just to become individual believers but are to be part of a Christian community. Christian faith and practice is a group trip, and congregations are one of the main realms in which discipling is to continue. I said my efforts to connect Hank to church near him were unsuccessful, and that's probably the biggest mistake I made. I talked with Hank about choosing and attending a local church, something he never took me up on, but I now think I should have also come at it another way, by contacting a church near him and asking them to make contact with Hank and invite him.

Here are a few principles about discipling that come from a curriculum offered by a Washington DC church:

- Discipling is *intentional* and *deliberate* — it is not something that just happens, it is the result of purposeful initiative on the part of other Christians.
- Discipling involves *encouragement* — Christians need encouragement in order to be faithful and to persevere in their faith.
- Discipling is focused on making followers of Jesus, i.e. *Christians* — not on just general moral reformation or even worse, copies of yourself.
- Discipling is ultimately rooted in the *word of God* — not just our good advice.

- Discipling is *loving* — to care for someone's soul in this way *is* love.
- And finally, discipling is *relational*; it involves more than just watching a lesson on video — it involves humans sharing our lives with others.[2]

I heartily agree with each of those statements.

Well, what might discipling look like? There's no set pattern, but there are several possibilities, and none of them require having a seminary degree.

A couple of them are indirect, such as praying for the person and doing our best to behave in ways that are consistent with our belief in Christ.

Some active ways might include some of the following:

- Inviting a new Christian to read a book of the Bible or a pertinent passage of scripture and then meet to discuss it one-on-one.
- Complimenting the person when they've made a conscious effort to live faithfully.
- Encouraging the person not to give up in the face of a failure to live their faith.
- Discussing together what you've both just heard in a sermon.
- Sharing your personal experience of "learning the hard way" what it means to follow Jesus.
- Attending a spiritual growth class or a new member training with the person.
- Showing up when the new disciple has a personal crisis or loss.
- Suggesting ways to interpret personal events in the individual's life as something other than judgment or expressions of God's disapproval.

There are more actions that help disciple someone, but these are some we can begin with.

And don't overlook that discipling can also take place in our home, where the things we speak about and model for our children, can, in fact, be ways we are fulfilling the Great Commission.

There's one more thing we should note from today's scripture reading. It tells us that when the eleven disciples encountered the risen Lord, "they worshiped him, but they doubted." There they were with the resurrected Jesus right in front of them and they experienced both an eagerness to worship and a reluctance to believe what they were seeing. Bible commentator Eugene Boring observes that this mix of awe and doubt "represents Matthew's own theological understanding of the meaning of discipleship, which is always a matter of 'little faith,' faith that by its nature is not the same as cocksureness but incorporates doubts within itself in the act of worship."

Boring also said, "'Doubt' here is not theoretical skepticism, but the risky wavering of the one who must decide when more than one possibility seems reasonable and right."

It is good for us to remember that when we are seeking to disciple someone that both we as the mentor and the other person as the learner are often wrestling with questions about what it all means and whether we are on the right track.

Thus, Boring concluded, "It is not to angels or perfect believers, but to the worshiping/wavering community of disciples to whom the world mission is entrusted."[3]

There's an old preacher story that makes a similar point. It tells of Jesus arriving in heaven after his ascension. There, he was greeted by another occupant of heaven who praised his faithfulness and work but then asked what arrangements he had made for his work to continue. Jesus responded, "Well, I have about 120 followers."[4] The other person looked at the 120 and said, "They look like a ragtag group, and not very promising. What's your plan if they fail?" To which Jesus replied, "They are my only plan. If my followers fail, there is no other plan."

So that's where we stand. God calls us to be faithful, and make disciples, counting on God himself to change their hearts and lives.

And in doing so, we should remember Jesus' words in this passage: "Go therefore and make disciples of all nations ... teaching them to obey everything that I have commanded you. And remember, I am with you always, to the end of the age."

Amen.

Proper 5
Matthew 9:9-13, 18-26

# Jesus The Initiator, The Responder, And The Waylaid

The lectionary gospel reading for today embraces two passages from the ninth chapter of Matthew, but they are not continuous. Another passage stands between them, and it's not clear why the lectionary committee picked the two that they did to stand together. What's more, the two chosen passages include three incidents, the second and third of which are miracle stories, but the first is not. Nonetheless, the three together show us Jesus interacting with people in three different ways.

In the first incident — the call of Matthew to follow Jesus and the meal that follows the call — Jesus was the *initiator*. He is walking along and sees Matthew sitting at his booth collecting taxes. Without any preliminaries, Jesus said to Matthew "Follow me." And Matthew got up and did so.

A dinner came next, and though the account in Matthew's gospel didn't tell us where the meal took place, the gospels of Mark and Luke, which also include this story, do. Calling Matthew by his other name, Levi, they explained that the dinner was at Matthew's house.

All three gospels reported that the other guests, besides Jesus and his disciples, were "tax collectors and sinners." That phrase lumped together two groups that good religious people did their best to avoid. Tax collectors were Jewish men who were employed by the Roman overlords to collect taxes from their own people, and the people suspected them of collecting more than was legally due and pocketing the difference. "Sinners" was an umbrella term that swept together individuals who were guilty of flagrant moral offenses and others whose "sin" consisted of laxity in observance of the food laws, tithes and religious rituals, as well as those who's very professions put them outside of the certain aspects of the law of Moses — for example, bankers, whose work involved lending money at interest, which was a violation of Exodus 22:25.

It may have been that this meal was in a courtyard of Matthew's house because somehow, some Pharisees, a strict group who scrupulously observed the Mosaic laws, saw the meal taking place, and asked the disciples, "Why does your teacher eat with tax collectors and sinners?" Jesus himself answered, "Those who are well have no need of a physician, but those who are sick. … For I have not come to call the righteous but sinners."

He wasn't saying that those, like the Pharisees, who thought of themselves as righteous had no need of the gospel message he brought, but rather that those who acknowledged their sin where in the right headspace and right emotional location to receive that message.

The Pharisees missed the point, however. Jesus associated with these marginalized people not because he wanted to be one of them, but to invite them to change their ways and enter the kingdom. It was Jesus functioning as the initiator. Had the Pharisees been listening to Jesus' explanation, they'd have understood that.

And that call was heard. At least some of the tax collectors and sinners Jesus associated with began to change their ways as a result of that association. If you track this "tax collectors and sinners" phrase in the New Testament, you'll find three things. First, the biblical tax collectors and sinners *listened* to Jesus. As Luke pointed out, "Now all the tax collectors and sinners were coming near to listen to him" (Luke 15:1).

But they went further. As a group, they were beginning to let the gospel penetrate their skepticism. Matthew told us that even because of John the Baptist's preaching, they *believed*. In

Matthew 21, we find Jesus saying to the chief priests and elders: "Truly I tell you, the tax collectors and the prostitutes are going into the kingdom of God ahead of you. For John came to you in the way of righteousness and you did not believe him, but the tax collectors and the prostitutes believed him; and even after you saw it, you did not change your minds and believe him" (Matthew 21:31-32).

Some tax collectors took the next step too: they *sought baptism*. Luke said, "Even tax collectors came to be baptized, and they asked him, 'Teacher, what should we do?" He said to them, 'Collect no more than the amount prescribed for you'" (Luke 3:12-13). Note that Jesus did not ask the tax collectors to leave their employment, but to conduct it ethically and honestly.

In the second incident, Jesus was not the initiator. A leader of the local synagogue (Mark and Luke tell us his name was Jairus) came and beseeched Jesus to come with him to see his young daughter, who had just died. No doubt having heard some stories of miracles Jesus had performed, Jairus held the hope that somehow Jesus would bring her back to life. Here we see Jesus as the *responder*. He agreed to go with Jairus, and they set out with the disciples and a crowd milling around them.

And that brings us to the third incident. While they were enroute to Jairus' house, a woman in the crowd, who had been suffering from hemorrhages for twelve years, reached out and touched the fringe of Jesus' cloak, believing she would be healed. Jesus sensed what had happened, and now we get to see Jesus as neither the initiator nor the responder, but as the *waylaid*. Here he was, on an important mission to help Jairus' daughter. Matthew had it that the girl had already died, but in Mark's and Luke's accounts, she was near death, which added urgency to Jesus' journey to Jairus house. And on the way, he was interrupted by this woman. Still, he took the time to speak kindly to her, telling her that her faith had made her well.

He then resumed his journey with Jairus, and when they got to the house, Jairus' daughter was indeed dead. But Jesus restored her to life.

Taken together, today's passages show us Jesus the initiator, Jesus the responder, and Jesus the waylaid. In each of these circumstances, Jesus dealt willingly and graciously with people where they were: Matthew at his tax booth, Jairus on his knees seeking help for his daughter, and the woman in the crowd touching his cloak.

No doubt, Jesus relates today to people in more modes than just these three, but these three are different enough from each other that they can help us visualize what it might mean to trust in Jesus and receive what he has for us.

It's likely that many of us here in church today at some point met Jesus the initiator. Perhaps it was in our youth, when at church or church camp, someone told us about Jesus wanting us to follow him, and we caught the vision. While the invitation came from a person, internally, it felt like Jesus taking the initiative and personally inviting us to be his disciple. That might have been a gentle experience — like the famous picture of Christ patiently knocking on our heart's door. Or it may have been a dramatic one. Some people have described the initial entry of Christ into their lives as him breaking through their defenses and storming into their heart, telling them to get comfortable with him because he was staying a while. I suspect Jesus' initial approach to us varies according to the readiness of our soul.

It's also likely that we've met Jesus the responder. How often have you prayed "Lord, help me!" and found that in some way, that help came. It's not that Jesus came to be at our beck and call, but still, there is comfort in knowing that he hears us when we pray, and that, as his response to Jairus' request for help shows us, compassion is a primary quality in the one we call our Savior and Lord.

But what about Jesus as the waylaid? That's a strong word, and one of its synonyms is "ambushed." Another is "detained." At first blush, those words don't seem very appropriate to describe the action of this woman, who, apparently feeling unworthy to approach Jesus directly, decided to do something that she probably thought he wouldn't even notice — touching the fringe of his cloak. But despite her intention, her action did interrupt, ambush, and detain Jesus. If you happen to have seen the dramatization of this incident on the steaming TV program *The Chosen*, you may remember that when the woman surreptitiously touched his robe, Jesus had a sudden physical autonomic response, almost as if he'd been strongly jolted by some force. I think those who staged that scene for the program got that response right.

In Mark's version of this incident, there are two uses of the word "immediately": Mark said that as soon as this woman touched Jesus' clothes, "*immediately* her hemorrhage stopped … and she was healed of her disease." And at that same moment Jesus was "*immediately* aware that power had gone forth from him" (Mark 5:29-30, emphasis added). Don't let anybody tell you that Jesus wasn't waylaid. But the two simultaneous "immediately" usages tell us that there was a significant involuntary response from Jesus that met the woman's need. And Jesus quickly thereafter, though waylaid, gave his approval to what happened by saying to the woman "Take heart, daughter; your faith has made you well."

What a strong hope that gives us, especially if we've never been in the Jesus camp, or we have but have since wandered away. We've either never had a connection to Jesus or we haven't had any connection to him in a long time. But then, something happens in our life, or in our thinking, that makes us feel the need, at least metaphorically, to touch his garment, interrupt him, present our problem, and seek something from him. This story of Jesus the waylaid, suggests that if there is enough faith to reach toward him, we can hope to hear him give his approval of our uninvited reach, his saying to us, "Take heart, daughter; your faith has made you well," or "Take heart, son; your faith has made you well."

Sure, that will only be a starting point, but it's at such starts that new life directions begin.

One reason we know that Jesus was willing to be waylaid was because of a parable that he himself told, the one we call the prodigal son. In that parable, a son demanded of his father his inheritance, which he received and then squandered in a location far from home. He was eventually impoverished with not even enough to eat. In his desperation, he decided to return home and ask his father if he could be a servant in the household, knowing that even the servants there were better off than he currently was. He set off for home, completely undeserving, but intending essentially to waylay his father with the request.

But you know the story. His father was eager to take him back, fully as a son, because the waylaid father experienced the lad's return as a moment of joy.

We have an expression in today's jargon that describes the son's decision in the far country to reach out to his father, and perhaps ironically, that expression is "a come-to-Jesus" moment. The term is often applied to situations where we have a moment of sudden realization, comprehension, or recognition that precipitates a major change in our lives, one that may or may not have something to do with spiritual matters. The actual term comes from Christian revival meetings in the nineteenth century that were literal calls for people to come to Jesus.

We are probably better to separate it from revival practices and simply understand it a wake-up call to reach out to the compassionate Jesus, whom we may have ignored until this moment, but to do so with the assurance that he welcomes being waylaid, even by those who have resisted all previous overtures from him.

Amen.

Proper 6
Matthew 9:35-10:8 (9-23)

# Feeling It In The Gut[5]

Several years ago, my wife Jeanine, who is an RN, went with a church mission team to Haiti on a work project. While other team members were there primarily to construct a school building, Jeanine went as the team nurse. When the church leaders in Haiti found out that the team coming in included a nurse, they asked if she would come prepared to teach a first-aid class to some of the clergy on the island.

Jeanine did that. Since the ministers spoke only Creole, she had to teach the class through an interpreter, but it worked out all right.

But why did members of the *clergy* want first-aid training? That's not training most pastors in the United States seek. You might guess that it had to do with a shortage of healthcare workers on the island nation, and that was part of the reason. But the rest of it had to do with belief. In that nation, many follow the voodoo religion. When they are sick, they call for the witchdoctor, a practitioner of that faith. When those same people hear the gospel and are converted to Christianity, they stop using the witchdoctor and turn instead to a practitioner of the Christian faith, the local pastor.

Say what you want, there is a certain logic to that switch, because the converts are bringing with them a worldview in which faith and health are closely connected.

It will help us in understanding today's gospel lesson to keep in mind that many people in Jesus' day held that same worldview. The text talks about Jesus teaching in the synagogues, announcing the good news of the kingdom, and healing every disease. Healing, it seems, was of one piece with the teaching and preaching. And the same was true further in the text where Jesus sent his disciples out to not just announce the nearness of God's kingdom of heaven, but also to "Heal the sick, raise the dead, cleanse those with skin diseases, and throw out demons."

We can also note from last Sunday's gospel text that Jesus, speaking in metaphor, referred to himself as a physician (Matthew 9:12).

In fact, we can't read any of the four gospels without witnessing Jesus spending a lot of time and energy healing people. Because he gave so much time to that task, we cannot dismiss it as having no bearing on us today, as if only what he *said* during that time works in the twenty-first century, but not what he *did*.

But even if you agree with that, you'll also probably agree that it's much harder to see the application of Jesus' healing activities to ourselves than it is to see the application of his teachings to ourselves. There are at least two reasons for that.

For one, we live in an age where medicine has developed clearly as a separate discipline from religion. We've all seen the miracles medicine can work. When you have a loved one who is seriously sick, you may well call the church and have that person put on the prayer list, but that's not all you do. You also seek professional medical care for them.

And the other reason we find it so hard to connect with Jesus' healing work is because of the so-called faith healers who are sometimes proven to be charlatans who are not really healing anyone. Such characters are an embarrassment to Christianity, and most of us want nothing to do with anything that resembles that in any way.

But none of that permits us to dismiss the healing activity of Jesus that all four gospel-writers record. And we should note that one of those writers was Luke, who was himself an actual physician. All the gospels, but especially Luke, use the expression "to heal" with reference to Jesus' mission. Listen, for example, to this verse from Luke 5: "One day, while [Jesus] was teaching, Pharisees and teachers of the law were sitting nearby ... and the power of the Lord was with him to heal" (Luke 5:17).[6]

To help us think about how Jesus' healing ministry applies to us who attempt to follow him today, let's make a few observations from the scriptures:

First, it appears that Jesus did not consider healing his primary mission. As we pointed out in last week's sermon, Jesus declared that his purpose of work was to "proclaim the good news of God ... saying ... 'The kingdom of God has come near,' and calling on people to repent and believe" (Mark 1:14-15).

Second, we get the impression that Jesus sometimes felt that the healing got in the way of his mission. Often, when he healed someone, he told the person not to tell anyone.[7] Several times, we find him leaving one town and moving on because the demand for him to continue healing in the first location had become overwhelming. Mark tells us about a time when Jesus had spent the day in Capernaum. At evening, sick people started coming to him, and he healed many people. The next morning, he went out to a deserted place to pray, but his disciples sought him out, bringing word that people were looking for him. Instead of going back with them, however, Jesus responded, "Let us go on the neighboring towns, so that I may proclaim the message there also; *for that is what I came to do*" (Mark 1:38, emphasis added).

And a final observation from the scriptures is that despite all the power at Jesus' disposal, he never used it to benefit himself. He never charged anyone for his help. He didn't heal to make himself famous — in fact, as we saw, he tried to keep his healing work quiet — and he did not use it to get himself down off the cross.

So, what can we learn from Jesus' healing ministry? Two things, I think, and the second is the more important.

The first is the significance that some people in Jesus' own day attached to it — basically that since he could perform such wonderful and helpful healing miracles, he was indeed the Son of God. John, the writer of the fourth gospel, followed that line of reasoning. As one example, John told of Jesus healing the son of an official in Capernaum — a long-distance healing since the son was not physically present. After narrating the healing, John comments, "Now this was the second sign that Jesus did after coming from Judea to Galilee" (John 4:54). A sign was an indicator or a signal of something.

I call this the less important learning from the healing miracles of Jesus simply because Jesus is not the only one in the Bible to perform healings. Some of the prophets did, as did some of the apostles. The mere fact that Jesus did some miraculous things, even if every one of them could be authenticated, may be *evidence* of his identity, but it is by no means *proof*, and it is seldom enough to build one's faith on.

But here's what I think is the more important thing: that by healing those who came to him, Jesus showed us that compassion was one of his primary characteristics, and by extension, it is a primary characteristic of God the Father, as well.

Remember that Jesus came into an age when to have compassion meant that you were going to feel bad a lot of the time. There was nothing approximating medicine as we know it, and for most people, to contract almost any kind of illness beyond those that the body could shake off by itself meant that you were doomed to suffer with it without any help. There were also no social services to help you live with it.

If you were a healthy person with even a modicum of compassion, your feelings would be assaulted every time you walked down the street, for there you see the blind, the crippled, the diseased, the maimed and others pitifully begging for alms. Your compassion might move you to toss a few coins in someone's cup, but beyond that, there wasn't anything you could do.

And you did what most other unafflicted people did. You tried to shut your feelings down and not look at the suffering all around you.

But then here came Jesus, who refused to ignore his emotions, who refused to avert his eyes from those who were sick and suffering. Several times in the gospels you will encounter this statement about Jesus: "He was moved with compassion."

The Greek word for compassion comes from the same root as the word for viscera, the bowels, the intestines. Thus, you can understand why people sometimes speak of feeling pity "right in the pit of my stomach," or saying, "It tied my stomach in knots."

When Mark told about a man with leprosy — a horribly disfiguring and disgusting disease if ever there was one, and highly contagious one to boot — coming to Jesus, we can assume that Jesus felt this man's agony right in the gut. The man said to Jesus, "If you choose, you can make me clean," Jesus stretched out his hand and *touched* him and said, *"I am willing"* (Mark 1:40-42, italics added). Do you see what a compassionate decision that was?

Now, do you understand why this is good news for us? I'm not talking about you and me demanding healing miracles, but about how good it is to know that the one whom we have called our master has, as a primary characteristic, the quality of compassion. I'm not suggesting that that means that he lets us off the hook for wrongdoing without our repenting of it, but it gives me great relief to know that God in Christ feels it in the gut for me, and that his first reaction to my woes and the messes I make in my life is likely to be compassion.

There's one other thing of importance to note here, and that is how Jesus' compassion has become a model for his followers. Think about how many hospitals, children's homes, helping agencies, nursing homes, mission aid centers, and, in earlier times, orphanages and "unwed mothers" homes, started as the work of churches or Christian groups. Yes, some of them have developed into secular agencies since, and some failed miserably at living out their mission, but most retain at least some of that sense of following the example of Jesus.

The compassion of Jesus also shone brightly in the lives of individual Christians as well, those who were trying faithfully to follow Jesus' example. Here's a story that comes from 1988, and the year is important only because it was a time before doctors had almost any medicines they could use in the battle against AIDS. Back then, to have that disease generally meant you were doomed to a short life of suffering and then death. I found the story in a news magazine, and it concerned people who opened their homes to take in foster children who were born infected with the AIDS virus. Many were the offspring of mothers who were drug addicts and had AIDS themselves.

For some of these babies, there was hope. By eighteen months of age, children normally lose the antibodies acquired from their mother, and about half the babies converted to HIV negative. When that happened, the babies were removed from those foster homes and moved to permanent situations to make room in the foster homes for more AIDS babies. The half of the babies who didn't get better stayed in the foster homes where they eventually got sicker and died.

Imagine if you were one of those foster parents — bonding with babies who were either going to die or be moved out. And then you were asked to repeat the process with new sick babies. Talk about needing to have compassion! It would hurt less if the care-giving adults would insulate themselves more — wall off their emotions — and not love the children, but you see, it was the love and compassion that was the redeeming feature for those children. Some of these foster parents even took in the birth mothers when they became too weak to care for themselves.

One of these foster mothers was named Helen, who was a Christian. At the time of the article, she was 41, a woman whom the writer described as "a matriarchal blend of sweetness and strength." Helen was caring for 21-month-old Denise, one of the babies who did not outgrow the AIDS virus. Helen explained, "All of us have a season. With Denise, we know we'll only have a season. But we make the most of what we have today. You just let the child blossom into your life. Let the joy come out."

The reporter described Helen playing patty-cake and singing to the little girl, and Helen explained that you "do all the mushy things that prolong a child's life."

Let me read to you the final paragraph from the article:

> A few weeks later ... the mushy things no longer suffice. The doctors have prescribed morphine for Denise's pain, and Helen has begun to sing, "Jesus loves me! This I know," as she rocks the child. "It's okay to go," she whispered. "These arms will hold you again." At the hospital soon after, with Helen and her husband and the birth mother all cradling one another and the child, Denise heeded Helen's sweet voice and died.[8]

By itself, the fact that Jesus healed some citizens of the first century doesn't mean much to us. But when you understand that he did that because he was unwilling to avoid the pain that caring about others would bring, and when you know that he is now the one to whom we turn, it suddenly means a great deal. And when you add to that the realization of how much good happens today because people are following him, it means even more.

Jesus was moved with compassion. Let us understand that part of being his disciples today means that we allow ourselves to be so moved as well.

Amen.

Proper 7
Matthew 10:24-39

# Rethinking Your Neighborhood

Chris Froome is a professional road racing cyclist who as of this writing, rides for the pro-cycling team Israel–Premier Tech. He has won seven Grand Tour races, including the Tour de France four times, as well as a host of other races. But while the Israeli-Hamas War was raging, it was Chris' wife Michelle who made news on the cycling websites as well as in general news media when she declared in a series of thirteen tweets on X (formerly Twitter) that Muslims are a "drain on modern society" and that "there are no innocent Gazans." She also wrote that Muslims were "here to take over" and that she was "sick of sitting idly by quietly supporting Israel while the Hamas propaganda takes over social media."

"Women's rights matter! Gay rights matter! Trans rights matter!" she wrote. "Hamas doesn't support any of those. Take the blindfolds off and see the reality of the hatred they are spreading. There are no innocent Gazans."

She went on to say, "Enough is enough! The silent majority needs to stand up and be heard. We don't want your religion, we don't want your beliefs. It is not compatible with modern civilization."

And she added, "This is not about cycling[;] it is about the world my children are being raised in. More parents need to be concerned about this."

Her posts came after pro-Palestinian activists called for "more protests than ever" against Israel-Premier Tech, the racing team her husband rides for. The protesters incorrectly refer to Israel-Premier Tech as being "Israeli government-sponsored," but it's not. Israel has no official connection to the team, but its co-owners are Israelis who formed the team in hope of bringing more Israelis into the realm of bicycle racing. Currently, however, none of the team members are Israelis.[9]

Some news media were quick to brand Ms. Froome's remarks as a racist rant filled with hatred and called it a "vile tirade,"[10] and she has since taken her X account down, but it struck me at the time that her comments weren't so much mean-spirited as they were indiscriminate, sweeping all Gazans and all Muslims into the same bucket. Certainly, the members of Hamas deserve some of her comments, but not everyone in Gaza is a Hamas supporter and not every Muslim is "here to take over."

But we can probably understand how her opinions have developed. Think about how often, especially since 9/11, the term "terrorist" has been linked to "Islamic." It's easy to forget that the terrorists who claim Islam as their faith are viewed as extremists by the larger Muslim world. And Michelle Frome is a mother of young children, so her concerns about the world in which they are growing up are understandable. None of that excuses her wholesale accusations against Muslims in general, but it helps us understand her outlook.

In the scripture reading for today, we find some Pharisees flinging indiscriminate accusations around too. Jesus alludes to that when he warns his disciples about coming persecution, saying, "If they have called the master of the house Beelzebul, how much more will they malign those of his household!"

Beelzebul was a name for Satan, and Jesus was referring to the fact that the Pharisees had said *he* was allied with Beelzebul. (You can read those charges for yourself in Matthew 9:24 and 12:24.) They were unwilling to acknowledge that when Jesus healed people he did so by the power of God, and they insisted that he was only able to drive out demons because he was in league with Beelzebul, the ruler of demons.

Those sort of undeserved associations happen today as well. Some observers have noticed that in online discussions, as they get longer, the chances increase that someone will make a comparison to Nazis or Hitler. In fact, one data analyst has analyzed 4.6 million reddit comments to find that 78% of conversations that reach 1,000 or more comments mention either Nazis or Hitler.[11] The point is that the comments are not discussing Nazi Germany or Adolf Hitler himself but are using those names to brand someone else — sometimes a US politician, but it can be anyone — as being like those twentieth-century evildoers. And the problem with that, of course, is that it trivializes the atrocities of Hitler and the Nazis during the Holocaust. If you want to reference them in historical discussions about World War II, that's fine. But using those words to insult someone today is almost always out of line.

But of course, that's Jesus' point in our text. In effect, he is saying to his followers, "If they call me the devil, just think of what they will call you." He was using that thought as a lead in to help them put the upcoming persecution in perspective about what they should really fear: not those who can kill their bodies but the one who can destroy their souls.

In our better moments, we really know that not all Muslims are extremists, not all politicians are self-centered, and very few people deserve to be compared to Hitler or Beelzebul. But it's easy to not do our best thinking.

We who read the Bible may recall that after Philip met Jesus, and then told his friend Nathanael that Jesus of Nazareth was the one Moses and the prophets had written about, Nathanael's first response was "Can anything good come of out of Nazareth?" (John 1:46). We recognize that that statement was not the result of clear thinking on Nathanael's part. It was stereotyping, and had Nathanael stuck with that viewpoint, he'd have missed out altogether on the opportunity to become a follower of Jesus. But fortunately for Nathanael, he took Philip up on the invitation to come and see Jesus for himself, and when he did, he realized that his dumping of everyone from Nazareth into one pot was just wrong.

Perhaps the realm where name-calling and stereotyping takes place with regularity today is in national politics. The vicious bipartisanism in Congress these days makes it easy for us who are not directly involved in political work to think of politicians in general as sleazy. And while there may be some who deserve that title, painting all politicians with the same brush contributes nothing except despair or anger regarding the political process.

But even for us who are not politicians, the bipartisan divide in the country tends to make us suspicious and distrusting of our fellow citizens.

Back in 2002, the late Charles Krauthammer, who self-identified as a conservative, but was often hard to nail down to any one ideology and was widely read by liberals as well, posted a column in *Townhall*[12] in which he said, "To understand the workings of American politics, you have to understand this fundamental law: Conservatives think liberals are stupid. Liberals think conservatives are evil."

Krauthammer's point was that both groups see the other as caricatures, though he didn't use that term in the column. A caricature is when certain characteristics of a person or a group are exaggerated to a comic or grotesque effect. But the trouble, as Krauthammer suggested, is that both groups treat the other as though the caricature is an accurate portrayal.

He said, for example, that when conservatives say liberals are stupid, they mean that "in the nicest way. Liberals tend to be nice, and they believe — here is where they go stupid — that most everybody else is nice too. Deep down, that is. Sure, you've got your multiple felons and your occasional war criminal, but they're undoubtedly depraved 'cause they're deprived. If only we could get social conditions right — eliminate poverty, teach anger management, restore the ozone, ... — everyone would be holding hands smiley-faced, rocking back and forth to 'We Shall Overcome.'"

Regarding liberals' view of conservatives, Krauthammer said, "Liberals are not quite as reciprocally charitable. It is natural. They think conservatives are mean. How can conservatives believe in the things they do — self-reliance, self-discipline, competition, military power — without being soulless? How to understand the conservative desire to actually abolish welfare, if it is not to punish the poor? The argument that it would increase self-reliance and thus ultimately reduce poverty is dismissed as meanness rationalized — or as Representative Major Owens, D-NY., put it more colorfully in a [then] recent House debate on welfare reform, 'a cold-blooded grab for another pound of flesh from the demonized welfare mothers.'"

No wonder politics includes so many episodes of "irreconcilable differences"! In the current political climate, some aspects of these caricatures may have changed or even flipped, with, for example, liberals thinking conservatives are stupid and conservatives thinking liberals are evil, but Krauthammer's primary point that we pigeonhole people who see things differently from us and assign them motivations that may be inaccurate or overstated remains the same.

But let's get closer to home on this. Virginia Heffernan, a political columnist at the *Los Angeles Times*, began her February 5, 2021, column[13] by saying, "Oh, heck no. The Trumpites next door …, who seem as devoted to the ex-president as you can get without being Q fans, just *plowed our driveway clean without being asked and did a great job.*" She then asked, rhetorically, "How am I going to resist demands for unity in the face of this act of aggressive niceness?"

She went on to posit her theory that this generous act was freely given because both she and her neighbors were white people in an all-white neighborhood. She backed this theory by quoting a line from an old Eddie Murphy *Saturday Night Live* sketch where Murphy declared, "… when white people are alone, they give things to each other. For free."

Heffernan next noted that historically, nice acts have sometimes been performed by unsavory parties, referencing Hezbollah's social outreach programs and French Nazi sympathizers who believed that Nazi soldiers were "polite."

That's a lot of freight to dump on neighbors whose only "sin" — in Heffernan's eyes — was to continue to be part of Donald Trump's "base." There was no indication that they had been among the people who stormed the Capitol on January 6, but she made it clear in her column that she was open to *them* making "amends" — "Not with a snowplow but by recognizing the truth about the Trump administration and, more important, by working for justice for all those whom the administration harmed."

Heffernan cited a comment from Senator Ben Sasse (R-Neb.) following the Capitol attack. "The United States," Sasse said, "isn't Hatfields and McCoys, this blood feud forever." And, he added, "You can't hate someone who shovels your driveway."

"So, here's my response to my plowed driveway, for now," Heffernan wrote. "Politely, but not profusely, I'll acknowledge the Sassian move. With a wave and a thanks, a minimal start on building back trust. I'm not ready to knock on the door with a covered dish yet."

We may not be able to do much about the state of the political scene, but Heffernan was talking about her *neighborhood*. And for her, the neighbor plowing snow from her driveway was an incongruity that didn't fit with the caricatures she had formed about "mean" Trumpites, and she was having trouble getting past it.

"Avoiding caricature" is a way of saying that we don't characterize someone with whom we disagree as a bad person simply because he or she sees things differently from how we do. And we certainly don't decide that all members of an ideological group are alike.

Except that sometimes we do. Sometimes even at family gatherings, we get involved in political or cultural conversations that leave us wishing we — or the other person — hadn't come to the meal.

Regarding those whose political view or ethnicity or theology or culture is different from ours, it takes some disciplining of our thinking to step over those barriers and remind ourselves that we are not the final authority on every matter. Like Heffernan, we may not be ready to show up at their door with a casserole, but we can recognize that a kind deed or a good word from someone else is a reminder that they are not fully defined — and perhaps not even remotely defined — by our mental image of their group.

Yes, there are evil people in the world. But we need to be careful how fast we are to assign that designation to people whom we simply don't understand or don't agree with.

I think the Lord wants better from us. It can start by trying to see our fellow citizens as whole persons rather than as representatives of a monolithic stupidity or a conspiracy of meanness. Or as Nazis or Beelzebul. Try "neighbor" instead. And you know what Jesus said about what his followers should do about neighbors.

Amen.

Proper 8
Matthew 10:40-42

# What's The Reward?

I have a friend who is a Christadelphian. The group is small enough — only about 50,000 people worldwide — that you may have never heard of them, but Christadelphians, which means "Brethren in Christ," are Christ-followers, noted for their deep commitment to reading and understanding the Bible and for their sincere application of moral and spiritual values. They preferred not to be called a denomination, since they hold a few beliefs that are different from the mainstream of the Christian faith, but they describe themselves as "a world-wide community of Bible students whose fellowship is based on a common understanding of the scriptures."[14]

I mention the Christadelphians here because of their intentional practice of hospitality within their group. On their online statement of faith and beliefs, they say, "It is our distinct beliefs and dedication to hospitality that have enabled us to survive as a separate community, though in most places we are quite thinly spread."[15]

As my friend explains it, "Christadelphians widely practice a form of hospitality where members are often welcomed into the homes of other members, *even if they have not met before*. This practice reflects our view of being a global family in Christ, extending fellowship and support wherever possible" (emphasis added).

My friend says he's stayed with dozens of families for a few days to three weeks all over the world, and that he and his wife have hosted dozens of families they have not met before the visit. The length of stay is generally based on the needs of the visiting members and the capacity of the hosting family, my friend says, "keeping in mind the primary purpose is to support the faith and fellowship among brethren, rather than for settling down."

He also says that "these visits often result in sharing and discussions around scripture, reinforcing our shared beliefs and encouraging one another in faith. It's a time of mutual edification and spiritual growth."

The theme of hospitality links us to today's gospel passage. The lectionary has had us reading from Matthew 10 over the past few weeks, but since each reading has been only a few verses, you may not have noticed that the whole chapter contains Jesus' instructions and cautions to his twelve disciples as he prepared them to go out two-by-two on their own missionary journeys to heal the sick and share the good news of the kingdom of God.

Today's passage contains Jesus' final words of instruction before sending them out, and though the instructions are limited to just three verses, their meaning is not immediately clear when we read them without having the cultural background that Jesus' disciples did. That background includes knowing about the *shaliah* concept of ancient Jewish practice, according to which, a person's duly authorized messenger is to be considered the same as the person sending the message.[16] The first *shaliah* inferred in the Bible is the servant in Genesis 24 who was sent by Abraham to find a wife for Isaac. Those receiving that servant understood that in doing so, they were in effect receiving Abraham himself, and so they were gladly hospitable toward the servant.

When Jesus said to his disciples, "Whoever welcomes you welcomes me," his followers got it right away. When people extended hospitality to these disciple envoys of Jesus, they were welcoming Jesus. What's more, when they received and embraced the disciples' message about the coming kingdom of God, they were receiving *Jesus'* message, and that is more likely what Jesus was hoping for.

The *Didache*,[17] a Christian document usually dated to the century after Christ, suggested that the wandering representatives of Christ should only be given hospitality for short periods of time, so that they would not settle down but continue spreading the gospel message.[18] That's obviously different from the Christadelphian practice, but I suspect that one reason for the *Didache*'s urging of short stays was because so many of the early Christians were impoverished. Without some form of welfare to help them, hosting a traveling Christian for more than a day or two was a true hardship for the hosting family. The *Didache*'s concern is not so much a problem in our time, but its focus on continuing to spread the gospel message is valid. Today, we can do some of that through technology channels, so physical travel for that purpose may not be as critical.

But Jesus added a second clause in the message to the disciples: "… and whoever welcomes me welcomes the one [that is, God the Father] who sent me." This statement isn't quite as startling to Jesus' disciples as his statement in John 14:7 surely was: "If you know me, you will know my Father also. From now on you do know him and have seen him." I can imagine some preacher with too strong an opinion of him- or herself saying, "whoever welcomes me welcomes the one who sent me." But I can't imagine that person saying, "If you know me, you will know my heavenly Father also."

But in the context of Jesus saying that whoever welcomes his representatives is welcoming him and his heavenly Father, Jesus reminded his hearers that even he was a *shaliaḥ*, an agent for God himself. It also reminds us that Jesus was actually present in or with his disciples. And we recall that one of the names for Jesus was Emmanuel, which means "God with us" (Matthew 1:23).

Jesus next said, "Whoever welcomes a prophet in the name of a prophet will receive a prophet's reward, and whoever welcomes a righteous person in the name of a righteous person will receive the reward of the righteous …." Essentially this is repeating his point using different language. The "prophet" in this sentence could refer to the disciples, but it also embraces the prophets of Israel's history, who often had their messages rejected or ignored. But Jesus was adding that those who do accept the message *receive the same reward as does the prophet*, which under the teaching of Jesus, is entry into the kingdom of God. Jesus also mentions that those who welcome a righteous person will receive the reward of the righteous, which surely refers to eternal life.

And then Jesus said, "… and whoever gives even a cup of cold water to one of these little ones in the name of a disciple — truly I tell you, none of these will lose their reward." In Matthew, the term "little ones" often refers not to children, but to humble or beginning Christians, who may also be poor. Such persons should be welcomed just as heartily as the "righteous person," which may represent "prominent" or "established" Christians. You may recall that Matthew developed this theme much more fully in chapter 25, when he quoted Jesus' words about caring for the "least of these" as in effect, caring for Christ himself.

The subject of hospitality is still clear in these statements from Jesus, but we now see that they are the groundwork for his comments about rewards — or what we might call *benefits* of following Jesus. As we've said, the reward Jesus was probably alluding to was eternal life in the kingdom of God. While that's certainly something we should want, there are some more immediate benefits of following Jesus as well. There are aspects of the Christian faith that help and sustain us right now, every day, in the daily course of our lives. The Old Testament writer of Lamentations knew this truth. He wrote: "The steadfast love of the Lord never ceases, his mercies never come to an end: *they are new every morning*" (Lamentations 3:22-23, emphasis added).

I've heard another testimony to the daily help of Christianity too. In a Bible study class where we were talking about eternal life, a woman volunteered that though she believed in heaven, that wasn't why she was a Christian. She was a Christian, she said, because of what Christ meant to her in the here and now. In fact, she went on to say that even if someone could prove to her that there was no afterlife, she would still want to be Christian.

What other more immediate benefits are there, daily blessings that God brings us through our Christian faith? I'm thinking here not so much of material things as of benefits to our emotions, character and spirit.

Naturally, we can name such benefits as comfort and help, guidance and example. But here are a few others:

For one, our relationship with Christ helps us in deciding the kind of person we are going to be. Richard Wurmbrand, a Rumanian pastor, tells of explaining Christianity to a young painter while the two were traveling on a train in Siberia. As Wurmbrand talked passionately about Jesus, the young man not only began to understand, but also found himself believing in Jesus. When the two parted, the man told the pastor, "I intended to steal something tonight. Everyone does, after all. Now how can I? I believe in Christ."[19] Becoming a Christian had begun to determine the kind of person the young man was going to be.

For many of us who have grown up in the church, such determinations may not seem as obvious. We've basically accepted the faith as we came to understand it and may not have thought much about how our embracing of Christ helped to mold us into people of high values and good character. But think about it now. How many bad things did some of your schoolmates do that you did not do because of your commitment to Jesus? How many times have you rejected opportunities for bigotry, theft, dishonesty, slander, and so forth because you belonged to Christ? And how many times have you done good deeds, reached out to help someone, given to worthy causes, accepted difficult assignments or been faithful to your spouse because you are a follower of Jesus Christ?

Help with who we are is a right-now blessing of walking with Christ.

Another immediate benefit of our faith is guilt relief. We may tend to think this is only for those who have committed great sins, but actually a great many people feel guilt over something from their past. In an English murder mystery novel, called *Brought to Book*, by Tom Heald, a detective's wife made this observation about guilt: "It was ever thus ... call Everyman and say "Flee — all is discovered" and there wouldn't be a man left in the country. They'd all be on the night [train] ... Mankind is a guilty secret waiting to be found out."

That may be an overstatement, but it's true for many. I know a man who says that for a long time he was haunted by something he did as a schoolboy, more than forty years earlier. Someone had stolen one of his textbooks. He couldn't face asking his father to buy another one, so he stole somebody else's. That continued to trouble him for a long time until as an adult, he confessed the matter to God in prayer and received forgiveness.

Lots of people continue to carry those kinds of things inside them. But the confession to God, and, where feasible, restitution to the person we've harmed, is the path to receiving God's forgiveness.

Still another daily life benefit of following Jesus is the matter of receiving direction for living. When Dr. C. Everett Koop was Surgeon General of the United States from 1981-1989, he became known for bold positions he took regarding health practices in America. One of these, which caused controversy at the time, was his advocacy of sex education as the most effective way to limit the AIDS epidemic. At a time when some people were still calling the disease a judgment from God, Koop, a deeply committed Christian, argued that candor and condoms were more effective public-health tools than sermons on chastity. He received a lot of criticism for that position, including from some highly placed officials. Koop was not against chastity, but he stated that as a public health officer, he had an obligation to help America control the AIDS epidemic. Though his views may not strike us as controversial today, they were then. His frank talk about the matter helped to change public opinion and, more importantly, public behavior.

But here's what I want you to hear. Koop saw a clear connection between his religion and the way he did his job. His faith provided him with direction. He put it like this: "I don't think you can ever separate your religious, ethical, or moral values from the way you do your job. There are social opportunities and obligations that go with sharing one's religion, such as compassionate care of the sick."[20]

Still another benefit is community and fellowship. We may not have the same in-home hospitality traditions as the Christadelphians, but we have the church, and it's a place where can be loved, supported emotionally, prayed for, and enjoy interaction with people who share our spiritual outlook.

And finally, there is one more immediate benefit of our faith, which I call "knowing whom to thank." A while back, a popular news columnist tried to imagine what the world would be like if everybody suddenly knew there were only 24 hours left to live. He concluded that the telephone circuits would be overloaded with desperate people trying to call family and friends to say, "I love you."

Likewise, it is important for our well-being as we live on this good earth to have somebody to thank for the blessings of life. As Christians, we know whom to thank, and that contributes to our contentment and inner peace.

Eternal life is a great destiny for Christians, and we have that to look forward to. But in the meantime, the Christian path of godliness is a good way to travel this life.

Amen.

Proper 9
Matthew 11:16-19, 25-30

# Wear The Light Yoke

Tina Fariss Barbour, a writer who lives in Virginia, has a form of obsessive-compulsive disorder (OCD) that includes obsessing about things she may or may not have done that could cause harm to others. While she now recognizes her mental illness and has learned ways to help her deal with it, for many years she tried to assuage her anxiety with compulsive actions and avoidance. And some of her OCD was related to religion. Barbour is a Methodist, but her obsession caused her to use religious practices in ways beyond what her church taught.

On her blog, "Bringing along OCD,"[21] she enumerated some of the symptoms she experienced at various points in her life since she was a child. Here are few from a longer list:

- Obsessed with sins I committed and the need for forgiveness from God. Along with that, obsessed about being "saved" in the fundamentalist Christian way. Compulsively prayed over and over to be forgiven and saved, then doubted that I got the prayer right.

- Obsessed with germs that might be on me and with the chance that I could spread them to others and hurt them. Compulsively washed my hands until they were red and raw, not wanting to touch doorknobs, not wanting my lips to touch a fork or spoon that someone else had washed.

- Obsessed with the cleanliness of bathrooms and seeing something that would repulse me. Compulsively cleaned, taking hours sometimes to clean a small bathroom. I didn't want anyone else to use my bathroom.

- Obsessed that I had hit someone with my car. Compulsively drove back and forth on the street, looking for a possible body.
- Obsessed with objects I saw lying on the ground that might harm someone else walking by. Compulsively picked up bent wires, sticks, paper clips, rocks, and the like, as I walked along.
- Obsessed with responsibilities I had and the fear that I could cause harm if I didn't do things right. Compulsively steered clear of responsibilities to others.

OCD comes in various forms and degrees, and in Barbour's case, the part that caused her to obsess through prayer and other religious practices is sometimes called "scrupulosity." The OCD Foundation says "Scrupulosity is a subtype of obsessive-compulsive disorder involving religious or moral obsessions. Scrupulous individuals are overly concerned that something they thought or did might be a sin or other violation of religious or moral doctrine. They may worry about what their thoughts or behavior mean about who they are as a person."[22]

Some historians have suggested that certain giants of Christian history, including Saint Ignatius of Loyola[23] and John Climacus[24] might have been afflicted with religious OCD.

In the *Autobiography of Benjamin Franklin*, he told of living at a boarding house in England in his younger years. There was another boarder, a single woman of seventy years, who lived up in the garret. As a young woman, she had lived in a convent somewhere in Europe and intended to become a nun, but for some reason, the country did not agree with her, and she returned to England. But she vowed to live as much like a nun as she could. Accordingly, she had given all her estate to charity, keeping only a small amount to live on, and then she regularly gave away even much of that, living on a watery gruel. She was so saintly that the owners of the house let her live there for free, deeming it a blessing to have her in the house. Every day, a priest came to hear her confession. Her landlady wondered how the old woman could possibly have anything to confess daily and asked her about it. The woman said, "Oh, it is impossible to avoid vain thoughts."

Scrupulosity is clinically defined as habitual doubt and anxiety about moral decisions, but that doubt and anxiety is usually centered around small details rather than large moral issues. The word "scruple" comes from the Latin word for a small, sharp pebble, like one might get in one's shoe.[25]

It is estimated that over three million adults in the United States have been diagnosed with OCD at some point in their lives.[26] OCD is treatable, however, and at minimum, sufferers can learn some methods to handle it. The religious aspects of scrupulosity, however, are a topic today's scripture puts before us, though Jesus' words on the matter apply to all of us who feel afflicted by an overactive conscience.

We will come back to that in a moment, but first, let's look at the gospel reading for today. It consists of three sayings from Jesus, each of which has merit and value on its own, but they seem to have no common thread to link them into one gospel lectionary reading.

The first of the sayings was Jesus' observation that there was no satisfying some people: "For John [the Baptist] came neither eating nor drinking, and they say, 'He has a demon'; the Son of Man [Jesus] came eating and drinking, and they say, 'Look, a glutton and a drunkard, a friend of tax collectors and sinners!'"

The second was Jesus' comment that the wisdom of God is hidden from some of those who are confident in their own wisdom, but it is revealed to some people who seem unimportant (I'm paraphrasing here).

And the third was Jesus' invitation to those feeling overburdened by life to take his "yoke" upon themselves, and to see how light it really is. This is the part of the reading we will focus on today. While it's applicable to Barbour's OCD, it has meaning for us all.

Just to remind ourselves, Jesus' third saying was, "Come to me, all you who are weary and are carrying heavy burdens, and I will give you rest. Take my yoke upon you, and learn from me, for I am gentle and humble in heart, and you will find rest for your souls. For my yoke is easy, and my burden is light."

The circumstances of Jesus' audience give us context for what Jesus said here. In that time, the Jewish people were under the heavy thumb of the Roman Empire, and in their daily rounds, they were at the mercy of Roman soldiers. They had to pay substantial taxes to the empire but had no say in how the empire operated. Their lack of freedom was a bulky load that added to the woes of their lives. And there was no real chance of escaping from the pressures of being a subordinate people.

But the demands of Rome weren't the only burden they carried. As Jews, especially those who wanted to live a life pleasing to God, they were additionally subject to the laws of Moses, which numbered 613 in the Hebrew Bible (our Old Testament). But in addition to those, many of the Jews of that day had been taught strict and legalistic interpretations of the Mosaic laws by the Pharisees and some rabbis. These interpretations created a body of requirements much larger than the original laws in the Hebrew scriptures. It was such a formidable mass of regulation that only a full-time legal specialist could hope to know them all.

The result was that the common people often unknowingly violated one of these interpretations. For those who were the most sincere and devout in their attempts to be faithful to the laws, a guilty conscience must have been a common experience. No doubt people were exhausted in their efforts to satisfy the demands of legalism. As a community of people, they shared the accusing conscience. And imagine what all that amounted to for those who like Barbour, suffered from OCD and scrupulosity.

Our circumstances today are different from those of the Jewish people of Jesus' day, but our weariness from some of the burdens we carry can leave us feeling just as exhausted. That's especially true regarding the political realities we live with. Publishing deadlines being what they are, I'm writing this during the run up to a presidential election, and the partisanship in the country is staggering. By the time you read this sermon, that election will be over, but, if recent political infighting is any gauge, the anger and venom in governmental arenas will continue, with many citizens aligning themselves with one side or another and the common good taking a beating. And all of that is very tiring.

Then there are the claims of religion on our lives, where churches and denominations split over social issues or biblical interpretation. Some of that disagreement also drains us. It may be that the uneasy conscience is more prevalent among those who attend church regularly than among the population at large, for we are people who really try to understand what it means to live righteously. The burden of undeserved guilt often comes to those who really try to do what they understand to be right.

Besides politics and religion, we find other ways that life weighs us down. We experience grief as a burden. We can feel heavy-laden with sorrow. If we have health problems, they can weigh on us. If we struggle with money, that can become a heavy burden. We know the weight of anxiety, of worry, and of fear.

Jesus did not promise to free his fellow Jews from the Roman occupation of their land or from the pain of being human. But he did offer spiritual rest. He was speaking to those who were trying to live holy lives under the enormous expectation that they keep all the rules the Pharisees had laid on them; they were the law-burdened. "Come to me, all you who are weary and are carrying heavy burdens, and I will give you rest," Jesus said, "for my yoke is easy."

A yoke was a device that enabled farmers to put an ox or a donkey to work pulling loads. The best yokes were custom fitted to the animal so it could work comfortably. Thus, when Jesus said, "Take my yoke upon you, and learn from me, for I am gentle and humble in heart, and you will find rest for your souls," he wasn't telling his hearers that they needed no yoke, no religious responsibilities, but he was saying that compared to the effort to live by every detail of the Mosaic law, following his way quite simple.

And we recall that in a different conversation, Jesus summarized the law with just two commands: 'You shall love the Lord your God with all your heart and with all your soul and with all your mind.' This is the greatest and first commandment. And a second is like it: 'You shall love your neighbor as yourself.' On these two commandments hang all the law and the prophets" (Matthew 22:37-40). The "law and the prophets" was a term for the Hebrew scripture, so this was Jesus' way of saying that living by those two commands, would fulfill what God wanted of them and would put them on the road of righteousness.

In short, Jesus was offering an exchange of yokes, swapping the heavy and clumsy yoke of religious legalism for the better-fitting yoke of love for God and love for neighbor. He certainly didn't mean that God's other laws had no value. But he did mean that the scrupulous attempt to reduce every law to a restrictive set of behaviors missed the point.

Jesus was addressing those who had felt inward moral disapproval, not because they were intentionally doing wrong, but because they were under constant judgment by nitpicking rules they couldn't even fully know. To paraphrase Jesus, he was saying, "Come to me, all you whose consciences bleed because you cannot achieve everything you believe is expected of you. And I will give you healing and inward peace."

To those in Jesus' day who were struggling to carry the heavy yoke of legalism, and to those of us today who are trying to carry the heavy yoke of righteous intentions, Jesus says, "Instead, carry my yoke. My yoke is easy."

We note that Jesus did not tell his audience that they needed no yoke at all, for unfettered freedom is itself a burden. We all need some boundaries to keep us out of trouble.

We started today by talking about scrupulosity — OCD focused on religion, However, it's important to move beyond the discussion of scrupulosity as a diagnosis. It is, perhaps, an extreme form of religious conscientiousness, but many Christians, without reaching such dysfunctional extremes, still wrestle with matters of a tender conscience and knowing at what point devotion to God goes beyond what God asks of us.

It would be good for us to consider how we use the words "must," "should," "ought" and the like, both with ourselves and when speaking to other Christians, as in statements that start, "To please God, I must ..." or "As a Christian, you ought to ...." Of course, there are some things that Christians must, should, and ought to do, but our reliance on such words to describe our religion may be a cue that we have allowed things to get out of balance in our spiritual lives, and that we have forgotten about grace, mercy and "come unto me, all you that are weary ...."

In fact, it would be useful to think about a double yoke. That's a collar made for two animals so that they can pull together as a team. The yoke of Jesus is not one he imposes on us, but one he wears with us. His words might be rephrased as "Become my yokemate and learn how to pull the load by working beside me and watching how I do it. The heavy labor of life will seem lighter when you allow me to help you with it."

All of that said, Jesus will not always take all our burdens away. Just as Jesus did not end Roman occupation, so Jesus does not always change our outward circumstances.

But he does give us the resources to keep going, and he teaches in this text that being conscientious in the extreme is not God's will for us, though God may use our struggles to build our character.

And we should take comfort that the yoke he does call us to wear is one of grace, mercy and peace.

Amen.

Proper 10
Matthew 13:1-9, 18-23

# The Emotional Gateway

When I was thirteen years old, I attended a church youth congress in New York City. During the worship service on the final day of the congress, an invitation was given for any of us who felt so led to come to the "mercy seat," the prayer rail at the front of the meeting hall, to ask God for forgiveness of our sins and to be "converted" and "saved."

There were well over a thousand young people in attendance. I have no idea how many "went forward," but it seemed like hundreds. In any case, as the altar call continued, I eventually felt compelled to go forward myself. I did so and knelt at the rail. Suddenly, I found myself sobbing uncontrollably. After a few moments someone knelt beside me and counseled me, and, I think, prayed with me.

When I later returned to my seat, I felt radically different. The only word that comes close to describing my feeling at that moment is "cleansed."

Surprisingly, I have absolutely no idea what the sermon was about that morning or who delivered it. I cannot remember who was sitting beside me during the service. I don't know who knelt to pray with me or even whether that person was a man or a woman. It may even have been another young person. I no longer remember.

Three things I do remember sharply: I cried, I felt cleansed, and I left that service with a commitment to Christ that was, I believe, real. In fact, I am convinced that my continuing relationship with Christ today had its active beginning at that prayer rail in New York.

I offer my own experience not because I think everyone else's commitment to Christ has to begin the same way. I firmly believe that some people become committed Christians by growing into their faith, accepting the gospel claims on them gradually as they are presented with them over years of Sunday school classes and church attendance. Others travel other paths. Not everyone has a sudden awakening.

But many people do. As I look back, I now realize that it was not my intellect or even primarily my will that led me to go forward in that meeting. It was my emotions. I have no doubt that the tone of that altar call (which I think lasted at least 45 minutes) created something of an emotional hothouse. And although I was surprised at the time by my tears, I seem to recall that many other young people were weeping as well. I went through a cynical period in my young adult years where I came to scorn the whole idea of altar calls. I began to refer to them disdainfully as "emotional baths" and became very suspicious about the faith of people who got emotional over their religious experiences.

A longer view, however, leads me to see that whatever excesses were present on the day of my conversion, the experience that my emotions led me into was genuine. Had my emotions not gotten snagged by the invitation that day, I might never have made the Christian commitment.

Nonetheless, reflection on my own experience and the experiences of many others I have witnessed during my years as a pastor confirm the fact that an emotional commitment, unless soon bolstered by commitments in other areas, is usually short-lived. That, I think, is one point Jesus made in the Parable of the Sower. Matthew recorded it this way:

> Listen! A sower went out to sow. And as he sowed, some seeds fell on a path, and the birds came and ate them up. Other seeds fell on rocky ground, where they did not have much soil, and they sprang up quickly, since they had no depth of soil. But when the sun rose, they were scorched, and since they had no root, they withered away.

Later in this passage, Jesus explained this parable to his disciples. He said that the rocky ground referred to one "who hears the word and immediately receives it with joy [*clearly an emotion*], yet such a person has no root but endures only for a while, and when trouble or persecution arises on account of the word, that person immediately falls away."

Jesus was not suggesting that our emotions are not to be involved in our surrender to God, only that the emotional surrender alone is generally not sufficient for an enduring relationship.

That is certainly true in other areas of life. A man and a woman meet and fall in love. They get an emotional high out of being in each other's presence. They feel intense pleasure being together and feel blue when apart. And sometimes people rush into marriage while still in the throes of these heady emotions. Later, when reality sets in and the feelings subside, they may be extremely disappointed in their choice of marriage partners.

Marriages that last and remain healthy must be reinforced by other things, like appreciation for who the other person really is, commitment to working on the relationship, respect for differences, a willingness to compromise and so forth.

As far as my early emotional surrender to God was concerned, I realize in retrospect that it was soon bolstered by at least three other things:

First, my parents were committed Christians. They consciously sought to behave in a Christian way in our home. They set an example that reinforced the commitment I had made.

Second, I regularly attended worship and other church activities. I had already been doing so, but those things became more meaningful. Youth Bible studies began to get my intellect involved. Faithful church attendance meant that I was regularly exposed to preaching, praying, hymn singing and the like. Many of my friends, including girlfriends, were church people.

Third, the denomination of my youth encouraged participatory worship and Christian practice. I was sometimes called on (without advance warning!) to pray aloud in church services. It was the practice in that denomination to give "testimonies" or "witnesses" to our faith in church, and I began to do that. I also helped in the social service and helping programs of the church. These things all involved me physically, mentally, and socially in various aspects of the Christian life.

The point is, by the time the emotional high wore off, other things had helped to get me firmly entrenched in the Christian experience.

In other areas of life, we do sometimes yield to the power of emotion. For example, have you ever driven all night in a snowstorm just to get home for Thanksgiving? Is your credit card bill at the end of the month the best reflection of your spontaneous nature? Have you ever given in to the overwhelming urge to call someone and when you did, you found out your presence was being sought?

But there is in all of us a natural tendency to resist opening our lives to God. Here our emotions can serve us well by allowing the inner security system against the call of God to be temporarily breached. If the breach can be widened by getting our intellect, social relationships, and other aspects of our being involved, then our emotions will have done us the great service of being the first highway for God to march down into our hearts.

This is not the first highway that God uses for everyone. For example, the great Christian writer C. S. Lewis told of his conversion, in which it was his intellect rather than his emotions that opened his heart to God. But for many of us, our emotions are the first force over the wall of our barricaded hearts.

Falling away from our commitment to Christ is one danger of letting an emotional commitment go unbolstered by other surrenders, but another danger is shallow religion. What can happen is that our emotional surrender is so joyful that we come to believe that the emotional high is the norm for religious experience. This can lead to silly beliefs. One might be the expectation that Christians should always be happy and that when they are not, they have lost their faith.

Shallow religion can also send us on endless quests to regain the emotional high. In years past it was a common practice in many churches to hold a "revival" every six months or so. While some good things happened in some of those, I have always wondered what we were trying to revive. Since revivals were usually attended by the very same people who were regular attendees of the church, perhaps it was the feeling of joyful excitement surrounding their initial conversion that they were trying to recapture.

Sometimes, when young people go to church camp, they experience an emotional and spiritual high that's so strong that they find it hard to leave for home at the end of the week. Many times, when I was involved in leadership at church camps, I saw kids break into tears as the camp drew to a close and the time to go home arrived. Those tears, in part, represented the pain of leaving the spiritual high point they had experienced.

Sometimes too, young people who have had an uplifting spiritual experience at camp return home and are disappointed that they cannot regenerate that same high week after week in their home church.

Yet something genuine happened to them that week too. The preacher-writer Frederick Buechner wrote, "When you are young, I think your hearing is in some ways better than it is ever going to be again. You hear better than most people the voices that call to you out of your own life to give yourself to this work or that work."[27]

But the fact is, there are times when we simply must walk the Christian walk by faith, not by feelings. I read somewhere about a helicopter pilot who was based on an aircraft carrier in the Pacific Ocean. During a blinding fog he was trying to make it back to the ship. He knew that he was flying at a low altitude, but the dense fog caused him to completely lose his sense of balance, a condition known as vertigo. In fact, it felt like he was flying the chopper on its side. But he had been trained to rely upon his instruments and for fifteen minutes he had to trust that the instruments were right even though everything felt wrong. The trust paid off and he landed safely. Many times, our feelings are unreliable in reflecting reality.

But having said all of this, we need to recognize that feelings do have an important place in the Christian life. We should not make feelings the prime ingredient in our faith, but we can recognize that God continues to use the emotions as a communication channel.

Perhaps it was for this reason that Jesus chose as his followers some passionate, turbulent people. At least one of them was even known as a "zealot." Jesus was not afraid of enthusiasm or passion. Indeed, he looked for the overflowing power of the heart in people. The evangelist Dwight Moody is quoted as saying, "I'd rather try to restrain a fanatic than try to resurrect a corpse."

This does not necessarily mean that we get all emotional about faith, although there is nothing wrong with that. But it does mean that we permit ourselves to be moved by the presence of God within us. It means that we allow ourselves to feel the things that surely must touch God. Certainly, God feels pain when people suffer or starve or abuse and kill one another. We need to be careful not to harden our hearts against that kind of pain. It is less painful to shut such things out of our thoughts, but unless we are willing to feel the pain God feels, then we can neither be fully Christ's disciples nor will we be inclined to do very much to bring an end to such wrongs.

Not all of us have the same emotional quotient. We are not all capable of the same depth of feeling, and that's okay. It's merely individuality. But to the degree we are able, we need to allow ourselves to feel those things that hurt people and then let that emotion move us to do what we can to stop unloving and uncaring things from happening.

But God also feels gladness and joy. Luke 15 contains the parables of the lost sheep, the lost coin, and the prodigal son. Read them with an open heart and you will see that each of them is about joy in heaven. In each case, when that which was lost was found, be it the sheep, the coin, or the son, the reaction from heaven was joy. God feels glad when anyone who is estranged from him is reconciled, and we can also. Not all of us have the same joy quotient. But to the degree we are able, we can let gladness motivate us to share the good news of Jesus freely and joyfully.

Imagine how empty a marriage would be if the partners did not open their emotions to each other. What would a relationship be like if we did not share our warmth and joy, and even our anger and depression with one another?

Some years ago, a group of German insurance companies did a study that showed that men who did not kiss their wives good-bye when leaving for work are more inclined to be moody, depressed, and disinterested in their jobs than the kissing husbands. Those who kissed their wives also tended to drive more carefully and lived up to five years longer.[28] This study suggests, of course, that the emotional response of a spouse has a bearing on the attitude of the other spouse, and surely that's a two-way street. In any case, the subject warrants continued testing by every couple!

A healthy spiritual life involves a lot more than just our emotions, but it certainly *includes* our emotions. We can learn to examine our emotional responses to what goes on around us and ask ourselves if we might not be hearing a call of God in what we are feeling. For some of us, emotions may be a prime gateway for God to connect with us.

What we do because of those feelings, however, is where the greater expression of our faith can be shown.

Amen.

Proper 11
Matthew 13:24-30, 36-43

# On Being Long-Tempered

The scripture reading for today includes two blocks of text. One contains the story Jesus told that we call the parable of the weeds among the wheat, and the other contains the allegorical interpretation of the parable Jesus gave to his disciples when they later asked him about it. Both blocks of text are from Matthew chapter 13, but the two do not appear in that chapter side by side.

By most counts, the gospels contain 46 parables from Jesus, and it's unusual for him to explain them. Most of the time, he just narrates the parable and lets the hearers draw their own conclusions about the meaning. That's fine with parables like the prodigal son and the good Samaritan, where the moral of the story is obvious, but some parables, like this one about the weeds among the wheat, are open to more than one lesson.

The weeds among the wheat is one of the very few parables Jesus interpreted, but it's notable that he told the parable — without interpretation — to a crowd of people who had gathered to hear him, but he later gave the interpretation only to his disciples. Thus, the second block of our text today begins by saying, "Then he left the crowds and went into the house. And his disciples approached him, saying, 'Explain to us the parable of the weeds of the field'."

That change of audience is important here, for it shows that Jesus was content for the general crowd to make what they would of the parable, but that he wanted his disciples to focus on a specific interpretation.[29] Some Bible scholars have noted that a change of audience sometimes seems to alter the lesson of certain parables.[30]

Today, we have a choice of whether we want to hear the parable as Jesus told it to the crowd or as he interpreted it for the disciples. If we choose the latter, it becomes an allegory about the final judgment. But if we choose the former, it can be for us a call for patience. Today, I have chosen to look at the parable as Jesus told it to the crowd.

Briefly summarized, the parable tells of a farmer who has planted good wheat seed in a field, but shortly afterward, some enemy of the farmer came and sowed weed seeds in the field as well. Bible commentators say the weeds were probably a type of darnel, which looks remarkably like wheat while growing but can be identified easily as darnel once it is ripe. As the two types of plants begin to grow, the farmer's crew notices the mixture and asks the farmer if he wants them to uproot the weeds. The farmer, concerned that the wheat will be uprooted as well, tells them to let both plants grow together and to wait for the harvest time to sort them out, and then burn the weeds and store the wheat in the barn.

As the parable stands, it can be about patience, which is what the farmer calls for. Wait until the harvest to sort the weeds out of the wheat.

I think it's worth our time to talk about patience, and here's why: Several years ago, I came across a communion liturgy written by the Scottish Bible scholar William Barclay.[31] I liked the fresh wording it supplied, so I decided to use it for the next time we had the Lord's Supper in the church I was then pastoring. I had it typed up so we could give a copy to each person.

Barclay included a prayer of confession in the service, and one of the things we confessed together was this:

> *In our homes*
> *We have been careless and inconsiderate.*
> *We have been moody and irritable and difficult to live with;*
> *We have treated those whom above all we ought to cherish with a discourtesy we would never dare to show to strangers;*
> *For this forgive us, O God.*

There was a lot more to the liturgy, of course, but after the worship service was over, several people mentioned to me that those few lines really hit home for them, and that they were indeed guilty of being "careless and inconsiderate ... moody and irritable and difficult to live with" and had sometimes treated family members "with a discourtesy [they] would never dare to show to strangers." In fact, I couldn't remember ever receiving as much reaction to a communion liturgy as I did to that one.

While those lines did not include the word "impatient," it's likely that impatience was at the root of a lot of the inconsiderate and irritable behavior going on in their homes, and I suspect that the same troublesome dynamic is afoot in many of our homes as well. I know impatience has sometimes contributed to inconsiderate and irritable behavior on my part in my home, and I too need to pray those lines of confession.

Patience, which we can define as "the capacity to accept or tolerate delay, without getting annoyed," or as "waiting without complaint" is not a particularly exciting topic, and I purposely didn't use the word "patience" in the title of this sermon because I didn't want anybody to tune out before I even began speaking. Nonetheless, patience is a topic that deserves to be talked about in church, particularly since in Galatians (5:22-23), the apostle Paul included it in the fruit of the Spirit list.

There's an old "Peanuts" cartoon that pictured the Lucy character — who was portrayed in the Peanuts world as having a difficult personality. This strip showed Lucy on her knees, praying. But then she jumped up and said to her little brother, "I was praying for greater patience and understanding, but I quit ... I was afraid I might get it."

We get Lucy quite well. Like her, we might feel we could benefit from some additional patience, but really, do we want it? We may like the image of ourselves as one who doesn't tolerate fools gladly, who doesn't sit idly by while there's stuff that could be accomplished and goals that could be reached, and who has enough edge to keep other people on their toes.

But impatience has its downsides, and many of them are nasty, and some are even deadly. Groups that track statistics tell us that, for example, road-rage incidents, many of which include the misuse of guns, are rapidly on the rise.[32] And even off the road, life is coarser when there's a me-first attitude in play.

Patience is part of what makes the world go round. People who are willing to invest in others and give them time to grow and mature are contributing to good things in our culture. Patience is really a matter of length, of putting in the time. I know a pastor who was a caring person with many fine qualities, but he had difficulty putting in the time with people who were long-winded and took too long — in his view — to get to the point. I noticed when others were talking to him, he had a habit of stating their point for them, trying to move the conversation along. I don't think he realized he was doing that, but I think that some of his parishioners thought of him as not caring about them, when, in fact, he really did. His lack of patience was undermining his pastoral ministry.

In that fruit of the Spirit list where Paul included patience as Holy Spirit given quality, the Greek word he used that is rendered as patience in English is *makrothumia*. That's a compound word: *makros* is the Greek for "long," and *thumos* is the Greek for "temper." Translated literally then, *makrothumia* means "long-tempered."

That's not a standard English word but the opposite of it — "short-tempered" — is. And we refer to someone who blows up easily as having a "short fuse" or having a "low boiling point." Patience is the opposite of all that, and in earlier English versions of the Bible, *makrothumia* was often translated as "long-suffering." That word communicated that there are occasions with others where we really have to put in the time. In fact, patience is often an expression of love.

Okay, patience is usually a good thing, but what makes it so hard to be patient? Psychologists tell us that one reason is something called the "egocentric predicament." That's the natural tendency to be immediately aware only of our own wishes, thoughts and feelings.

For example, when we are waiting in a checkout line in a busy store, we would probably agree that everyone in the line is equally entitled to reach the cashier, have their items totaled and bagged and then depart. In fact, we believe that most of us would not push other people out of the way so that we could check out first. However, we are intimately aware only of our own feelings and needs, which naturally want to put ourselves at the head of the line so we are not inconvenienced — sorry about the rest of you.

The reason the egocentric stance is called a "predicament" is that it's a blind alley. It's very hard to see things from someone else's point of view. And it's even harder to see someone as God does. It's also a predicament because none of us struggle with the same weaknesses and thus, we don't easily understand why someone can be so foolish, bullheaded, anxious, annoying or whatever word you want to use to characterize them.

Is there a cure for impatience? There is, but, of course, it requires *patience* to get there. The reason Paul called patience — or long-temperedness — a fruit of the Spirit is that it is a virtue accessible through prayer. That's not likely to be a quick-fix process but prayer is the place to begin reviewing our shortcomings in that area and ask for help. And it can't be the prayer that says, "Make me patient, O Lord, and do it right now."

Ironically, some of the help may come in the form of more problems to solve and more difficult experiences to go through. But as James the biblical writer puts it, "Consider it a sheer gift, friends, when tests and challenges come at you from all sides. You know that under pressure, your faith-life is forced into the open and shows its true colors. So don't try to get out of anything prematurely. Let it do its work so you become mature and well-developed, not deficient in any way" (James 1:2-4, *The Message*).

May we be willing to take the time to grow in faith, and to be containers for the fruit of the Spirit.

Amen.

Proper 12
Matthew 13:31-33, 44-52

# Bringing Out Of Our Christian Treasure What Is New And What Is Old

In May of 2024, at its denomination-wide legislative gathering, the United Methodist Church repealed its rule against "self-avowed practicing homosexuals" being ordained or appointed as clergy within their church. The ban, which had been in place since 1984, was removed by a vote 692-51, without debate. The United Methodists also approved a proposal to allow, but not require, its clergy to officiate at same-sex weddings.[33]

These changes came on the heels of a split within the denomination where about a quarter of its US congregations withdrew, with many of them joining together to form a new denomination committed to traditional theology and practices.

During the same week that the United Methodist Church moved in this progressive direction, an article appeared in a national media source which reported that some US Roman Catholic congregations were "taking a step back in time."[34]

According to *AP News*, some parishes are in turmoil as traditionalism is resurging in the US Catholic Church. The upset is heightened because in the locations where the move back to earlier ways is occurring, it seems to be undoing much of the modernization the Catholic Church brought about since the Second Vatican Council (Vatican II) in 1962-1965. Pope John XXIII called that council because he felt the Catholic Church needed updating to better connect with people in an increasingly secularized world.

In the wake of Vatican II, generations of Catholics became used to and welcoming of the liberalization in their church. But in this new trend, while conservatives in the US Catholic Church are still a minority, their influence was growing.

In the parishes where the changes are evident, contemporary music is often replaced by music from medieval Europe. Sermons are focused more on sins and confession. Masses include more Latin. Some members of those parishes describe what's happening as "a step back in time."

Many American Catholics are not traditional in their outlook. Some support abortion rights and use birth control, and as their churches become more conservative, they have moved to more liberal parishes or have joined Protestant churches or have stopped attending altogether. But some Catholics prefer the more traditional approach.

Even Pope Francis worries about the American Catholic Church. While he has held the line on church dogma, he has pushed the global church to be more inclusive and has expressed more liberal views on same-sex relationships and divorce. Speaking to a group of Jesuits in 2023, he said that the US Catholic Church has "a very strong reactionary attitude," and added that "being backward-looking is useless."[35]

But those Catholics who support the conservative moves say that time will prove the critics wrong. They do not look at themselves as backward-looking at all, but as being more faithful to the Christian truth.

The changes in both the United Methodist and the Roman Catholic churches serve as a backdrop for something Jesus said in our gospel reading for today. The passage includes four parables from Jesus, each of them intended to communicate something about "the kingdom of heaven," which is Matthew's term for the kingdom of God. According to things Jesus said elsewhere in the Gospels, that kingdom is coming in the future, with his return, as for example in Matthew 24:30: "Then the sign of the Son of Man will appear in heaven, and then all the tribes of the earth will mourn, and they will see 'the Son of Man coming on the clouds of heaven' with power and great glory."

But he also talked about that kingdom being already present with him. At the beginning of his ministry, he said, "The time is fulfilled, and the kingdom of God has come near ..." (Mark 1:15). On another occasion, Jesus was asked by the Pharisees when the kingdom of God was coming, and he answered, "The kingdom of God is not coming with things that can be observed; nor will they say, 'Look, here it is!' or 'There it is!' For, in fact, the kingdom of God is *among* you" (Luke 17:20-21, emphasis mine). The best thinking among Bible scholars is that both ideas about the kingdom — yet to come and already here — are true. The kingdom has begun and is present in the hearts of Jesus' followers, but it isn't here in its fullness yet.

Well, we certainly know that. Political partisanship and social divisions are so strong in our country that what has happened with the United Methodists moving in a theologically and socially progressive direction and some US Roman Catholics moving in a theologically and liturgically conservative direction are examples of some of those more widespread divisions.

But in the four parables in our reading, Jesus didn't *describe* the kingdom. Instead, he used comparisons, similes: "The kingdom of heaven is like ...." In these parables, he tells us the kingdom is like a tiny seed that grows into a great tree; it is like a tiny yeast that leavens the entire day's baking; it is like a treasure hidden in a field; it is like a pearl that person wants so badly that he will sell everything else he owns to purchase it. These parables are all about the kingdom of God within us. We who follow Jesus possess the seed of the kingdom, the yeast of God's love, have the treasure of the Good News, the message that is valuable beyond all others. These parables are all about the kingdom of God that is here now, among us.

There is one more short parable in the passage we read from Matthew this morning: the net that catches fish good and bad, followed by a great sorting. That is talking about the kingdom to come. In the fully come kingdom, the security of its citizens is assured because those who refuse to live by the kingdom's love and graciousness will be excluded from it.

At the end of those parables, Jesus asked his disciples if they had understood what the parables taught about the kingdom of God, and they said "Yes." Jesus seemed to have accepted their reply, for he made this comment: "Therefore every scribe who has become a disciple in the kingdom of heaven is like the master of a household who brings out of his treasure what is new and what is old."

He was in effect comparing his disciples to the religious scribes who spend their lives studying the Mosaic law and the commandments. That is the background the disciples, as Jews brought up in the synagogues, bring with them, Jesus was saying. But when they came to Jesus and learned about the kingdom of heaven, they were able to put that together with what they already knew and thus bring out of their existing-plus-new knowledge the best of what is old and what is new.

The Bible scholar William Barclay helps us here by explaining, "Jesus never desired or intended that people should forget all they knew when they came to him; but that they should see their knowledge in a new light and use it in a new service. When they do that, what they knew before becomes a greater treasure than ever it was."[36]

In the midst of our divisions today, we need to hear Jesus' saying that "disciple[s] in the kingdom of heaven [are] like the master of a household who brings out of his treasure what is new and what is old."

You see, in politics, in social justice issues, in love-your-neighbor matters, and especially in our churches, we should not be expending much energy arguing over whether progressives or conservatives or can really be Christians. The answer is "Yes, they can." And we should not be tossing slur words at each other with conservative Christians calling progressives ones "woke" or "socialists" or progressive Christians calling conservative ones "bigots" or "Nazis." We who follow Christ, no matter how we express that in worship, have so much good we can bring from the past in common as well as so much creativity we can bring to new issues today that we need to learn to pull together. There are treasures, Jesus said, in both "what is new and what is old."

In fact, we need the best of what conservatives and progressives bring forth from their treasures. We need Christians who take seriously the fall of humankind and who recognize the impossibility of establishing paradise here on earth. We need Christians who believe in the necessity of personal salvation and of living righteously. At the same time, we need Christians who are "woke" in the best sense of that word, who are sharply aware of social injustice and are willing to tackle it.

We even need the differences expressed by the words "conservative" and "progressive." As individuals, we differ in our personalities, our sensibilities, our understandings and our experiences of life. Some of us find deep meaning in evangelical church worship and some of us find it in mainline church worship. We benefit both from those who view the Bible as God's final word on how we should live and those who see it as laying out divine principles on which we build as we wrestle with new understandings of the range of what it means to be human. We need people who are comfortable with not having all the answers and do not feel it necessary to defend God against all comers.

From both directions — the old and new, the conservative and progressive, we can arrive at a personal experience of faith that leads us to trust God and to follow Jesus. And from both directions, we can view each other brothers and sisters in Christ.

One of the attendees at the denominational legislative conference where the United Methodists changed their official stance toward same-sex people was Reverend Randy Frye, who is a life-long doctrinally conservative pastor within that denomination. But he was one who chose not to leave the United Methodists when many other churches and pastors did. He is the senior pastor at a United Methodist church in Kingsport, Tennessee. When he returned from the conference, he told his congregation that "nothing had changed," that the First Broad Street Church they love would continue to welcome people, show hospitality, and offer multiple ministries "because that's who we are."

The United Methodist legislative meetings — called "General Conferences" in their denominational lingo — occur every four years, and after each one, they come out with a new addition of the *Book of Discipline* that includes all the new legislation as well as the old, which continues unchanged. The restrictions on same-sex persons were added in the 1972 edition of the *Discipline*. As Frye saw it, all the most recent conference did was to "go back to the 1968 *Book of Discipline* which said nothing about human sexuality."

Frye also said that the new language affirming marriage between an adult man and woman or two adults "creates space for people like me who hold a more traditional view and for people who don't," Frye said. "It says we can be in the same church. We don't have to be fighting over that. So, I can live with that."

The most important message for United Methodists, Frye said, is to stay focused on discipleship. In The United Methodist Church, the mission is to "make disciples of Jesus Christ for the transformation of the world," as the denominational mission statement puts it. "That's where our energy and effort has to be," Frye said.

"I've been a conservative pastor in a liberal denomination my entire ministry," said Frye. "I've never felt like I didn't get an appointment [to pastor a United Methodist church] because of my theological stance. I never felt like I wasn't welcome because of my theological stance. And now, I can live into this new reality and help my church live into it, too."

Frye is realistic yet hopeful about the days ahead for The United Methodist Church. While he suspects some members of

First Broad Street Church, where he pastors, will leave because they can't abide with the current *Book of Discipline*, he doesn't expect an "exodus" of members. "Most of our people are coming to First Broad Street because this is their church. They want to be part of the ministries here. They're not 'one issue' kind of people, they're just not," he said.[37]

Those are wise people. May all of us within the wider church that grew out of the life and teachings of Jesus Christ learn to value the treasures, old and new, that our fellow Christians bring to life and worship today.

Amen.

Proper 13
Matthew 14:13-21

# Jesus, And The Wisdom Of Strategic Withdrawal

The passage that proceeds today's gospel reading tells about John the Baptist being beheaded by Herod Antipas. It also reports that when Antipas heard reports about Jesus, he said to his servants, "This is John the Baptist; he has been raised from the dead, and for this reason these powers are at work in him." It's likely that Antipas wasn't saying that Jesus was literally John come back in the flesh, but that he meant his comment in the sense of "Jesus is another John I'm going to have to deal with."

Thus, today's passage begins, "Now when Jesus heard this" — the news about John and Herod's declaration about Jesus — "he withdrew from there in a boat to a deserted place by himself." The fact that Antipas had killed John did not by itself pose a threat to Jesus, but Herod's fear that the powers at work in Jesus were similar to those John had employed was a threat against Jesus. So, according to Matthew, Jesus *withdrew* from the place where he was.

Greek is the original language for the New Testament, and the Greek word for "withdrew" is *anachoreo*. That same verb occurs three times in eleven verses of Matthew 2, and each time, the withdrawal was a response to a dangerous situation. (In English translations of Matthew 2, *anachoreo* is not always translated as "withdrew," but whatever word is used implies a withdrawal.) In 2:12, the magi were warned in a dream not to return to Herod (this was "Herod the Great," the father of Herod Antipas). The magi withdrew to their own country. In 2:14, Joseph was warned by an angel to flee with his family to Egypt because Herod was searching for their child, to destroy him. Wisely, Joseph obeyed and withdrew from Bethlehem to Egypt. And 2:22 tells us that later, after Herod the Great died, Joseph made plans to move back to Judea, but after being warned in a dream that Herod's son, Herod Archelaus, was ruling in Judea in his father's place, Joseph instead withdrew his family to Galilee.[38]

Given that Jesus' withdrawal in the face of Antipas' threat was to an isolated place to pray, we should not view it as cowardice. Nonetheless, it did remove him from a place where he had been sighted by many and thus was findable by Antipas. So, in terms of the effect his withdrawal had, it was more like a case of picking his battles. Getting arrested by Antipas would have sidetracked his mission — even if Herod did not have him killed — and so Jesus removed himself temporarily from the public eye.

The gospels show us several examples of Jesus using withdrawal as a tactic to keep his mission on track. For example, in Matthew 12, when Jesus learned that some Pharisees had conspired on "how to destroy him," Jesus withdrew to another area where he healed many people, but he also told them not to broadcast what he had done (vv. 14-16). That request was not out of fear of the Pharisees, but due to his concern that his healing work sometimes sidetracked his teaching mission. And other times, he withdrew from places where he had healed people, and he did so because the growing crowds seeking healing over-occupied him.[39] He was compassionate, so he had a hard time saying "no" to the ill, but he had a mission from God his Father to complete.

It doesn't take much imagination to see that the practice of withdrawal was a necessity for him. Jesus wisely recognized that he simply could not endure and succeed with his divine mission if his ministry was a constant, never-take-a-break effort.

In that age, when medical knowledge and practice was at a primitive level, most people had some ailments that could not be treated by the physicians of that day, and many were too poor to pay for medical help in any case. If Jesus had been willing, he could have spent all his time curing people. He sometimes withdrew to another place simply to husband his time and energies so he could stay on mission. Jesus' withdrawal was not a coldly calculated act — the fact that he could so easily be pulled aside to heal people testifies to that — but he had to make choices to accomplish the work God had given him.

The fact that Jesus himself used withdrawal as a way to pick his battles recommends that tactic to us who follow him. And we can learn from Jesus when such a move is likely to be helpful. Jesus withdrew when staying around for confrontation was premature or pointless, and there are times when we should consider doing the same.

Sometimes, withdrawal means physically walking away, but sometimes it can be refusal to participate in a no-win situation or conversation. During the run-up to the last presidential election, when there was a lot of strong partisanship among Americans, my friend Jack had an experience that illustrated this: He had gone to a local restaurant and ordered some take-out food. While waiting for his food to be prepared, he sat down in an empty booth. Almost as soon as he did, a man seated by himself in the next booth, attempted to start a conversation, by asking, "Well, what do you think about how they're running our country these days?"

"What do you mean?" Jack asked, and in response, the man said, "Well, son," and then launched into a tale about immigrants ruining the country and how it was the fault of the current administration in Washington. Jack was pretty well informed, and he recognized some inaccuracies in the man's claims, but the fact that the man clearly was enjoying his tirade, coupled with the fact that though he appeared to be about the same age as my friend, he continued to refer to Jack condescendingly as "son," communicated that this man was not open to having a real conversation, but rather wanted someone to echo back his own distorted views.

Jack chose instead to say, "I'm happy to talk to you, but not about politics." But that led the man to say, "Son, you better pay attention to the real news in this country; the major networks don't tell you the truth," and he continued his lecture. Jack simply turned away. The man apparently got the message, because he stopped talking. Soon, Jack's food was ready, and as he exited the restaurant, he said to the man, "Have a nice day." The man responded, "Yeah, you too, son. But pay attention to the real news." Jack just kept walking. Of course, he wanted to get his food order home while it was hot, but his leaving at that point was also a strategic withdrawal.

That was an encounter between two strangers, but we are more often likely to benefit from polite withdrawal in tense situations with people we love. Sometimes it may be wise to simply say "I'm not prepared to discuss this right now, but give me some time to mull it over," thus gaining time to pick our battles or proceed with the discussion later when we're prepared to speak about it calmly.

Notice that one difference between Jack's encounter with the stranger and the ones we may have with a loved one is that in Jack's case, his withdrawal was close to avoidance. He didn't know the other man, and they were unlikely to meet again. Having the discussion then or putting it off until later would probably have made no difference, so Jack essentially chose not to engage, which was almost certainly the right decision. But avoidance in conflicts with people we live with may leave the person's complaint festering and do damage to our relationship. So temporary withdrawal is more a matter of timing than avoidance.

You can even schedule when you will re-engage, saying something like, "Look, I'm exhausted right now, but I can see we need to talk about this. Can we have coffee together tomorrow morning?" The scheduling assures the other person that you are taking him or her seriously and gives time for both of you to look at the issue without the heat of immediate conflict. Scheduling also keeps you from procrastination, which is a quite different and less helpful force than strategic withdrawal.

Obviously, not every issue lends itself to the scheduling plan. Some things are so urgent and critical that they must be dealt with immediately, and part of wisdom is the ability to see the difference between the immediate need and the ones that can benefit from some withdrawal time.

Our gospel reading for today is nine verses long, and all this time, I've been talking about a single word — "withdrew" — from the first verse, so let's look for a moment at the rest of the passage.

As it turned out, Jesus' withdrawal to an isolated place in the face of Herod's threat put him in another unintended situation. Though he'd departed by boat on the Sea of Galilee, somehow the crowds figured out where he'd gone, followed him on foot around the shoreline and sought him out. Jesus, compassionate as ever, ended up curing the sick among them even though that wasn't his primary mission.

Then, because it was late in the day, and the people — 5,000 men plus women and children — needed food, Jesus turned the meager supplies at hand, five loaves and the two fish, into a filling meal for everyone there.

This miracle, usually shorthanded as "The feeding of the 5,000," is reported in all four of the gospels. In Matthew's telling of the story, the version we read today, it ends with the gospel writer's report about how large the crowd was. The very next sentence, which was not included in today's reading, tells that Jesus sent his disciples away by boat, dismissed the crowd, and withdrew to a mountain by himself to pray. In Matthew's timeline of the events, it appears that Jesus was simply resuming what he'd been trying to do before the crowd tracked him down — retreating to pray. And that was certainly part of his intention. But when the gospel writer John narrated this same story, he added a critical detail at the end of it: "When Jesus realized that [the crowds] were about to come and take him by force to make him king, he withdrew again to the mountain by himself" (John 6:15). The people had witnessed Jesus' ability to heal the sick and feed the hungry, so why not make him their king?

Yes, Jesus had come to announce the kingdom of God and invite people into it, but had he allowed them to attempt to make him an earthly king — even if such a move could have succeeded in the face of the power of the Roman troops that patrolled Galilee and Judea — it would surely have sidetracked Jesus from the work that God the Father had sent him to do. What's more, to view Jesus as king in the realm the people had in mind would cause them to miss altogether the message of God's love and grace Jesus had come to announce and demonstrate. He strategically withdrew from the crowd. In the end, of course, he did become a king of another sort, only then, his "throne" was the cross.

Withdrawal is not the solution to every conflict or claim on our energy and attention, but as Jesus demonstrated, it is a helpful practice some of the time, and as such, it deserves our consideration.

Amen.

Proper 14
Matthew 14:22-33

# Out At Sea With Simon Peter

Today's gospel reading follows immediately the account of Jesus feeding the 5,000 on the shore of the Sea of Galilee. When that event was over, Jesus dismissed the crowds and directed his disciples to get into a boat and head for the other side of the water, and he went up a mountain to pray. While the disciples were on the sea, a bad storm came up, and while it raged, Jesus came walking toward them on the water.

You who have been coming to church for a while have likely heard that story before. Three of the gospel writers — Matthew, Mark, and John tell it, but only Matthew added the part about Peter stepping out of the boat and walking on the water toward Jesus.[40]

That scene, with Jesus on the water and Peter walking toward him, was dramatized for us in the final episode of season three of the streaming video series *The Chosen*. I haven't particularly cared for some other media presentations about Jesus, but I must admit that *The Chosen* is an exception, and I heartily recommend it to you. There are two things about the show that I especially like: One is that it makes Jesus more accessible to today's audiences than any other media attempts I have seen…and the other is that while it stays close to the gospel accounts of Jesus, it fills in some plausible back stories that help us understand some of the puzzling things we encounter in the gospels.

At this point in Peter's life, he is still called Simon and his act of getting out the boat during a bad storm and attempting to walk on the water toward Jesus is certainly one example of *The Chosen* providing a backstory. What in the world was Simon thinking that caused him to attempt this dangerous act? Remember that according to Matthew's account, having Simon walk on the water wasn't Jesus' idea; it was Simon's. When the disciples first saw Jesus walking on the water, they were terrified. Real people can't walk on water, so they didn't believe it *was* Jesus and thought instead that they were seeing a ghost. But then Jesus spoke, saying "Take heart, it is I; do not be afraid."

But the disciples still weren't convinced, and who can blame them? Simon called out and said, "Lord, if it is you, command me to come to you on the water." And Jesus gave him permission to do so. Simon appeared to be trying to prove that the figure they were seeing really was Jesus, but was walking on deep water a logical way to do that? What if it *wasn't* Jesus but some apparition just claiming to be him? What were Simon's odds of surviving his stunt then?

*The Chosen* not only provided a plausible reason for Simon's behavior in storm, but also transmitted a powerful message of faith.

*Spoiler alert!* I'm going to tell you Simon's backstory and use the accompanying faith message as the theme for this sermon.

*The Chosen* started building Simon's backstory in the previous episode. You may remember from your reading of the gospels that at one point Jesus healed Simon's mother-in-law.[41] So the writers of *The Chosen* assumed Simon must have had a wife, and they named her Eden. Then they envisioned that while Simon was away with the other disciples spreading the news of the kingdom of God and healing the sick, Eden, who had conceived a baby with Simon before he left on his trip — but didn't know she was pregnant until after Simon left — had a miscarriage. Thus, when Simon returned, he noticed her glum mood and perceived something was wrong. Eden didn't immediately tell her husband what had happened, and Simon assumed it was something he had done, but he didn't know what.

But when he eventually learned of the miscarriage, he started to grieve and became resentful toward Jesus. Here, he had seen Jesus heal all sorts of people, including curing some from a distance, and Simon had been right out there helping, but Jesus hadn't done anything to keep he and Eden from losing their child. And their mutual grief became a wedge between the couple, so that they weren't even able to comfort each other. That upset was very much present when that episode concluded.

The final episode of that season of *The Chosen* opens with a quick journey back to the time of King David, who with one of his wives, is listening with approval to a performance of Psalm 77, which is about crying out to God in the midst of trouble. The next scene returned to the time of Jesus, and we soon find Simon, reluctantly with the other disciples and Jesus, and even being surly with his companions and Jesus. He is present with them at the feeding of the 5,000 and goes with the others in the boat afterwards, where they eventually see Jesus, walking toward them on the water.

Meanwhile, back at Simon's house, Eden's friends, including Mary Magdalene and the mother of James and John also noticed her gloom, and she finally confided in them about the miscarriage and her grief that would not heal. Her two friends decided Eden should visit the synagogue and hear God's word, and they accompanied her there.

When they arrive, the synagogue leader is solicitous toward Eden, and read to her Psalm 77, which is a prayer of desperation that eventually turns toward remembering the deeds of the Lord. He also suggested that Eden prayerfully immerse herself in the ritual bath, which is a large cistern of water in the synagogue that is used for ritual purification.

At that point, the footage cuts back and forth from Eden descending into the ritual bath and Simon, who is out at sea in more ways than one, attempting to walk on the water and managing a few steps. Cutting back to Eden, we see her asking God not to let Simon go, and then submerging herself into the bath even as Simon sinks into the sea. Jesus extends his hand to Simon and pulls him up. Simon ends up embraced by Jesus with both of them standing on the water. In the back and forth of the scenes, Simon and Eden re-emerge from their separate water experiences at the same time. We, as viewers, get the sense that they've both been embraced and pulled out of their downward spiral by Jesus.[42]

A later scene in the episode shows Simon coming home to a joyful reunion with Eden.

After Jesus rescued Simon from the sea and was holding him in a strong embrace, Simon said, "Don't let me go." Jesus assured him he would never do that. And that's when it dawned on me that the faith message underlying the Simon-Eden story is that when bad things happen to people who love God and trust Jesus, *Jesus is still there with them.*

Thankfully, the show didn't try to cook up some script lines trying to explain the unexplainable — why bad things happen to good people. There was no attempt to justify God or to give grim comfort by saying God allowed their child to die in utero because he needed another angel.

I've been a pastor for more than fifty years, and in that time, I've seen some good, faithful people experience some terrible blows that broke their hearts. I've officiated at funerals of a stillborn infant, a fourteen-year-old boy who choked to death, a recent high school graduate who joined the Army and died on the battlefield the next year, a newly married man who died leaving a young wife and child behind, a few who took their own lives, and many other burials. I've seen people suffer painfully from disease before death finally took them. Shortly after I moved on from one church I pastored, three young people who had been part of the church young group when I was there died in separate incidents: one in a house fire, one by heart failure, and one by homicide. My father, who was also a pastor, once had to conduct the funerals of two small children — siblings — who drowned in a pond. He did it, but it was hard for him to quell his own tears while trying to speak words of comfort to the grieving parents. Some of the painful things I've witnessed as a pastor have left me in tears, as well.

In all those years, I've never found an explanation for why bad things happen to good people. And I've noticed that not even the book of Job, in which undeserved suffering is the primary topic, has an answer either. That book calls us to trust God, but it doesn't explain why life can hurt so much.

That's where the Simon-Eden storyline in *The Chosen* comes out as well: No answers, but only the assurance that God will not abandon us to our tears and grief. Or as the apostle Paul said in Romans: "For I am convinced that neither death, nor life, nor angels, nor rulers, nor things present, nor things to come, nor powers, nor height, nor depth, nor anything else in all creation will be able to separate us from the love of God in Christ Jesus our Lord" (8:38-39).

Of course, Simon and Eden didn't have the words of Paul, who in their day had not even been converted yet, let alone writing the letters that eventually became part of the New Testament, but they did have the Hebrew scriptures, and may have learned from Psalm 77, which *The Chosen* used as a backdrop for the Simon-Eden crisis story.

The psalm begins in misery and despair:

> *I cry aloud to God,*
> *aloud to God, that he may hear me.*
> *In the day of my trouble I seek the Lord;*
> *in the night my hand is stretched out without wearying;*
> *my soul refuses to be comforted.*
> *I think of God, and I moan;*
> *I meditate, and my spirit faints.*
> *You keep my eyelids from closing;*
> *I am so troubled that I cannot speak.*

The psalmist goes on like that through the first ten verses. One Bible commentator observed that although those verses have the character of a prayer for help, they were not addressed to God directly, except for the single line "You keep my eyelids from closing," which sounded to me to be accusing God of keeping the psalmist from even having the relief of sleep. The commentator notes that it "is as if the psalmist has become so discouraged that prayer has become impossible."[43] Indeed, the psalmist said, "I am so troubled that I cannot speak."

At verse 11, however, there is a change in tone, where the psalmist at last does address God directly:

> *I will call to mind the deeds of the Lord;*
> *I will remember your wonders of old.*
> *I will meditate on all your work*
> *and muse on your mighty deeds.*
> *Your way, O God, is holy.*
> *What god is so great as our God?*

Here, it's likely that this transition is not an achievement of the individual psalmist, but rather it's that he or she is taking part in a communal process of remembering God's great help and "mighty deeds" in the past. Making this affirmation along with other worshipers about God's help becomes for the sufferer the beginning of healing. The previously mentioned commentator observes that "Psalm 77 issues a call to decision. In every age, the people of God are called to proclaim and to embody the reign of God amid circumstances that make it appear that God does not reign."[44]

In fact, we Christians are a people of hope built on the memory of what God has done for us in the past. That's no guarantee against the possibility of deep loss and bad things happening to us in the present, but the memory that God will not let us go, and that nothing can separate us from his love, can show us a way out of despair.

Proper 15
Matthew 15:(10-20) 21-28

# Faith Is A Verb

In my early years in ministry, I attempted several times, in the course of writing sermons, to come up with a good definition of *faith*, and in those early years, I was never satisfied with the results. It eventually came to me, however, that the problem was that I was thinking of faith as an *ability* — specifically an ability to believe in and trust God. The difficulty with that was that while I knew a lot of Christians who seemed to have that "ability," I also knew quite a few who, while staying within the church and participating in its missions and ministry, were more aware of what they doubted than of what they believed.

I even came across a verse from the apostle Paul that apparently supports that view: Romans 12:3: "...I say to everyone among you not to think of yourself more highly than you ought to think but to think with sober judgment, *each according to the measure of faith that God has assigned.*" (italics added). As I read it, Paul is saying that faith is something that God gives us — and *in varying amounts*. Could he be saying that some of us are given a great ability to believe while others are issued a smaller measure? The NIV wording of the same verse can be read as supporting that interpretation: "... think of yourself with sober judgment, in accordance with *the faith God has distributed to each of you*" (italics added).

Of course, it's possible that Paul meant that God gives the same-sized portion of faith to all, but that doesn't fit with the numbers of Christians who are "born believers" and the numbers who are "born skeptics." Whatever Paul's intent with those words, I am convinced that the ability to believe easily is not something we can just muster up on command. For some things, either you believe it, or you don't.

The problem, I now think, is that "ability" is a noun — a thing — and faith, while also always a noun in English, sometimes functions more as a verb — an action. Perhaps we'd get that better if the English had a verb form for faith ... maybe "faithing." We don't have such a verb in English, but it's significant that in New Testament Greek there is both a noun and verb form of faith: *pistis* is the noun and *pisteuō* is the verb. The verb form appears, for example, in Matthew 21:22 (CEB): "If you have faith, you will receive whatever you pray for". Note that "have faith" functions as a verb.

I am not saying all this to argue English syntax, but to make the point that when we act in faith, it is something we *do*, not merely something we *have*. And perhaps more to the point, in the gospels, Jesus did not talk about faith so much as respond to it when he saw it in other people, as happens in our scripture reading for today. There he said to the Canaanite woman who had asked him to heal her daughter, "... great is your faith!" She had not declared her allegiance to some theological doctrine, but she had vocally *wrestled with Jesus* (a verb phrase) to receive what she needed.

Keep the idea of faith as a verb in mind as we proceed.

The gospel story found Jesus in "the district of Tyre and Sidon." That was across the border from where most Jews lived. It was Gentile territory. If you read this story in context, you get the idea that Jesus went there to temporarily escape the pressure of the crowds that gathered around him everywhere he went. Yet, even here in a Gentile region, Jesus could not escape notice. And one person who hears of his arrival is a Canaanite woman — definitely not one of Jesus' own people. She had a daughter with a desperate problem. In the way that problem was understood in that day, she was being "tormented by a demon." Today, she'd likely be diagnosed as having some form of mental illness or possibly as suffering from epilepsy. Primitive medical knowledge in her day, however, had no treatments for such ailments. But her mother heard Jesus was in the area and sought him out, asking him to heal her daughter.

Jesus' response to the woman was not at all typical of his usual response to people in distress. In fact, at first, he did not even answer her. But when she persisted, he finally said, "I was sent only to the lost sheep of the house of Israel." In other words, "My mission is to the Jews." The Bible assures us that Jesus came to save any who would follow him, but apparently, he saw his mission in terms of planting the message with the Jews first and then letting them take the message to the world. But in making that comment at that moment, Jesus seemed to be again turning a deaf ear to this woman. "This woman and her daughter are no concern of mine at this time," he seemed to be saying.

At that moment, the woman knelt in front of Jesus, begging for his help, and he said something that sounded especially harsh: "It is not fair to take the children's food and throw it to the dogs." In that day, Jews sometimes referred to people who did not worship God as "dogs," though in the original Greek, the word Jesus used here was not the one for wild dogs of the street, but the pet dogs of the house, so it was not quite as harsh as it sounded in English. Still, the meaning of Jesus' answer to her was probably something like, "You are asking me to give you what is intended for my own people."

The mother, however, answered with a quick wit, saying, "Yes, Lord, yet even the dogs eat the crumbs that fall from their masters' table."

At that, Jesus remarked that the woman had great faith, and told her that the demon had left her daughter. The woman went home and found her daughter lying on her bed, completely recovered.

Frankly, Jesus' initial response to this woman is puzzling. Earlier in Matthew, Jesus did make an exception for a Gentile—a centurion—who wanted Jesus to heal his servant, and Jesus appeared far less reluctant to help in that case.[45] What's more, in that incident, Jesus declared "I tell you, many will come from east and west and will take their places at the banquet with Abraham and Isaac and Jacob in the kingdom of heaven" (Matthew 8:11), clearly a reference to Gentiles coming into God's kingdom. So, our puzzlement about Jesus' seeming disinclination with the Canaanite women remains.

We can learn from the whole story, however, that, although Israel is still Jesus' priority at this point in his ministry, he was willing to make exceptions, especially for a demonstration of exceptional faith. He was more concerned with matters of the heart than with ethnic boundaries. And Jesus now demonstrated that by making an exception to his own rule that he was to reach out only to the lost sheep of Israel.

Martin Luther was well aware of the seeming crudeness of Jesus' dog remarks. Commenting on this passage, he said, "[The woman] catches Christ with his own words. He compares her to a dog, she concedes it, and asks nothing more than that he let her be a dog, as he himself judged her to be. Where will Christ now take refuge? He is caught."[46]

But Luther took comfort in the fact that Jesus still hadn't shut the woman off completely. He was quick to point out that Jesus' answer was still "undecided and pending." What Jesus finally did, in response to this courageous woman's persistence, was the right thing. He didn't let his off-the-cuff answer stand. He pivoted, acting in a deeply merciful and loving way.

So, let's not dwell on Jesus' dog remark. He didn't try to explain or justify it himself. Why should we?

What is most remarkable is Jesus' declaration to the woman, "Great is your faith." Such faith can occur from unexpected sources.

Artificial intelligence is all the rage these days. You may not remember now, but the first AI program to be released was from the company OpenAI. They called it ChatGPT (which stands for "Chat Generative Pre-trained Transformer") Though technology has advanced since, back when ChatGPT was new, it was a wonder in that it could answer questions, respond to requests and give information in a form that simulated human dialog backed by a reasoning mind. It was, in fact, an artificially intelligent online conversation partner (a "chatbot" in tech jargon)

So I decided to test it out, and I asked ChatGPT *"How can the Christian faith be understood as a verb?"*

Here's ChatGPT's answer:

> "In the context of the Christian faith, understanding faith as a verb involves actively engaging with one's beliefs and putting them into practice. Here are a few ways that this might look in practice:
>
> **To believe:** As a verb, faith in Christianity involves choosing to believe in the teachings of Jesus and the Bible, even when they may be difficult or challenging to accept. This might involve studying scripture, attending church, and engaging in conversations with others who share one's faith.
>
> **To act:** Christian faith as a verb requires more than just belief — it also involves putting that belief into action. This might involve participating in acts of service, volunteering at a local church or charity, or working to promote social justice and equality in one's community.
>
> **To trust:** Trust is also a key component of faith in Christianity. This might involve trusting in God's plan for one's life, even in the midst of difficult circumstances. It may also involve acknowledging one's own limitations and recognizing that there are some things that are beyond our understanding or control.

"Ultimately, understanding Christian faith as a verb involves actively engaging with one's beliefs and living them out in tangible ways. It involves seeking to deepen one's understanding of God and his teachings and using that understanding to make a positive impact on the world around us."[47]

That's a decent and serious answer to my question. It was hard to grasp that my dialogue was with a computer, not a human being. But, of course, AI, then as now, draws its information from the world of information real people have already written or spoken about online. AI essentially scrapes and crawls the web, although since ChatGPT's beginnings, additional sources for AI's knowledge database have been added. But my point is that AI wasn't inventing new information about faith as a verb, but it was able to recognize in existing material written by humans when faith was being described as an activity rather than only an intellectual acceptance of certain doctrines limited by what Paul called the measure of faith that God has assigned. Sometimes faith is a verb because it involves choosing to believe even in circumstances where it is not an ability and it doesn't come naturally, as the AI answer suggests.

Sometimes the faith that matters looks like a woman, pleading with Jesus for healing for her daughter, and having the guts and gumption to switch the meaning of Jesus' dog analogy and so that he could perceive how deeply committed she was to getting even the crumbs of Jesus efforts to help her daughter become whole. That was faith in action.

Come to think of it, maybe that was Jesus' intention all along, to put the woman in a spot where he could see if she had enough faith for his healing of her daughter to be effective. In the end, there seems to be a pleasant surprise in his voice, when he says to her, "Woman, great is your faith! Let it be done for you as you wish."

Amen.

Proper 16
Matthew 16:13-20

# Your Key To The Kingdom[48]

Several years ago, I pastored a church in Bellevue, Ohio. At one point during that time, Earl Bruce, who was then the famed football coach at Ohio State University, came to the town to give an inspirational talk at a public meeting. After his speech, the mayor presented Bruce with a key to the city to indicate that the citizenry felt honored to have the coach in our community and that he was being given the status of "very important person."

These days, giving a key to the city is a symbolic gesture, but it dates back to medieval times when walled cities had gates that were guarded during the day and locked at night. But a key to the city might be given to someone the city fathers trusted as a friend of the city residents. The key was a functional one that would actually open the city gates.

Of course, few cities these days are contained within walls, but cities still give keys to esteemed visitors, residents, or others the city wishes to honor. The key given now is an ornamental, nonfunctional one that does not unlock any real door in the city, but giving it announces that the figurative "doors of the city" are open to the guest. All the same, the key does not endow any actual authority in terms of management of the municipality.

Sometimes, however, the giving of a key does indicate a certain measure of responsibility. Each time I was appointed to a new church, someone in the congregation would give me a key to the church building, which I took to indicate some actual authority, for with it came the duty of pastoring the congregation that worked and worshiped in that edifice.

In one church, it was the custodian, who was also a trusted member of the congregation, who gave me the key. He also had his own key to the building. His key conveyed a different set of responsibilities than mine, but it symbolized authority for him to carry them out, nonetheless.

Jesus had a God-given authority to announce the coming of the kingdom of God. His continuing authority sets him above and beyond all others, and that makes him the one we can follow with confidence. But there is another aspect of Jesus' authority. It comes up in the incident at Caesarea Philippi recorded in today's gospel reading. The time is late in Jesus' ministry, after the disciples have been with him for several months, long enough for them to have seen many examples of Jesus' authority in healing, teaching, example and so forth. It is also near the time when Jesus would begin his final journey toward Jerusalem and the cross.

It is probably because Jesus knew what lay ahead that he needed to know where his disciples were in their understanding of what they've been involved in with him. So, he asked, "Who do people say that the Son of Man is?"

The disciples answered, John the Baptist, Elijah, Jeremiah, or one of the other prophets.

But then Jesus asked the question behind the question: "But who do *you* say that I am?" Simon, probably speaking for the whole group, responded, "You are the Messiah, the Son of the living God." Jesus then said to him, "You are Peter, and upon this rock I will build my church, and the gates of hades will not prevail against it. I will give you the keys of the kingdom of heaven ...." (This is the reason, by the way, that in popular tradition, Saint Peter is considered the doorkeeper at the pearly gates.)

It is in these words that the matter of Jesus' authority comes up. Jesus was using symbolism similar to the "keys to the city" concept. He was honoring Simon, whom we also know as Peter, for his faith, but he was also giving him authority to open the kingdom to others.

The bestowing of authority was a vital necessity for Jesus. It is clear from the gospels that by this point, Jesus knew what was going to happen to him in Jerusalem. Since he was not going to be physically present with his disciples much longer, he needed them to carry on his work. Someone has to have authority to speak for the kingdom of God, but someone also has to have the responsibility to carry on Jesus' work of opening the kingdom doors so that people can come in.

This is the reason for Jesus' pleasure over Simon's recognition of Christ's lordship. Peter's birth name was Simon. But in this moment at Caesarea Philippi, Jesus called him Peter. It has been claimed by some commentators that Peter, which means "stone," had not been previously used as a proper name prior to Jesus giving it to Simon.[49] I can't verify that, but I do know that in Bible times, when a person was given a new name, it often signified a change in function. No longer was this man to be only Simon, the disciple. Now he was Peter, the apostle, a person authorized to open the kingdom of heaven to others. And upon the rock of faith authority, Jesus would build his church.

But was this function to be Peter's alone? It's true that Peter was singled out here, but Jesus' words to the disciples over the subsequent days made it clear that this responsibility of "carrying the keys" to the kingdom — at least insofar as it means the authority to introduce others to Christ — had been given to them all so that they and those who came after them in the faith could open the doors and let people in. In fact, Jesus' final instruction — about making disciples of all nations — was spoken to the whole group of apostles.[50]

As the church spread, the apostles did just that. They introduced others to Christ who in turn did the same for yet others. The authority to make disciples continues to be handed on, right down to today. In fact, this sort of authority might be described as the right to "author" others into the faith, and it comes to us today who follow Jesus. We, each Christian one of us, have a direct commission from Christ to author others into the faith.

There is an old story — probably not a true one, but it makes the point about the authority vested in us by virtue of our accepting Christ. According to the story, there was a woman who had held power in her church for years. Now elderly, she was not impressed when the church hired a new pastor who was only 25. When she was introduced to him, she harrumphed and said, "Young man, how can I possibly learn anything from you?" He replied, "Madam, when I speak to you, I am 2,000 years old." When it comes to inviting people into the kingdom of God, every Christian is 2,000 years old.

Of course, not every authority is granted to us. One that is not is the right to define the content of Christian faith and practice without reference to the church and what it has learned from Christ down through the centuries. But the responsibility to open the doors of the kingdom of God to others is given to us. Keys are meant for opening things that are locked, and every Christian is given a set.

The church has institutionalized the matter of authority in the ordination of clergy, which in some Christian groups, primarily Catholic, Orthodox, Episcopal, and Anglican, is called "apostolic succession." In those churches, the idea is that there is an unbroken line of continuity between what took place between Jesus and Peter at Caesarea Philippi 2,000 years ago and clergy today, a continuity preserved by an unbroken succession of bishops laying hands on clergy at the time of ordination. Most Protestant churches haven't focused as much on a continuity of bishops — indeed, not all Protestant groups even have bishops — but they have emphasized a continuity of message and gospel with the apostles. But in either case "apostolic succession" means that what takes place among Christians today is directly connected with this incident in our gospel reading involving Jesus and Peter. The fact that apostolic succession is used in clergy circles as an explicit grant of authority to pastors, however, does not mean that Christian laity do not have a divine commission to share the faith. In fact, that authority to open the doors of the kingdom of heaven is implicit in every Christian's faith.

As you probably know, years ago when many churches were building their parsonages, they often built them right next door to the church. But the truth is, most pastors prefer not to live so close, and one reason is that when they do, they often become by default the keeper of the key to the church. Every pastor can tell you stories about getting phone calls to "go over and open the church." Sometimes these are no problem at all but other times they are quite inconvenient. Back when I lived in a parsonage next to the church I was serving, I received a call once from a woman who wanted the church opened at 7 am on a Saturday morning, the only morning all week I allowed myself to sleep in. A minister I know who eventually left the ministry told me that one thing that confirmed his decision to leave was a call he got late at night during a snowstorm from a member who wanted him to go over to the church right then and open it.

Fortunately, most church members are more considerate than that, and some pastors handle the matter by making sure that everyone who needs to get into the church is given a copy of the key. In fact, one pastor said he thought that every member who is received into the church should be given a key right along with their membership certificate.

In terms of our buildings, that may not be practical, but there is a sense in which that is what happens when you declare your faith in Jesus Christ. You may not receive a key to the church building, but you do receive a kingdom key. Those are issued to every Christian, not just to pastors.

The fact is, however, many of us find it difficult to carry out this authority to author others into the faith. Parents sometimes have a difficult time using that key with their own children. Yet children are much more likely to embrace the Christian faith when they see it lived out before them in their homes and hear it spoken of there. Some parents rely instead on the pastor or some church program to spark their children's faith. Ideally, the church should supplement the home's witness of faith, but not replace it. One thing that helped me as a Christian was that

I heard the adults around me, including my parents, talk about their faith.

We usually find it even harder to author faith in another adult. We might go as far as telling the pastor that so and so needs a visit, but how often will we accept the authority granted in our own confession of faith to open the kingdom doors for that person? I'm not talking about going out and cornering strangers, but I am talking about using the opportunities God provides.

I read somewhere about a woman who ate her lunch at the same diner ever workday, and she almost always had the same waitress, so naturally, they chatted occasionally. The woman was a Christian, and that influenced her attitude and spirit. One day, the waitress said to her, "You are always so friendly, and you usually look happy. How come?" At first the woman responded with a glib reply, "Oh, it's just such a nice day." But then she said, "A couple of years ago, I had a spiritual experience. I met the living Christ, and I have been happier ever since."

These are the sort of stories where we'd like a tidy ending, saying that as a result of the woman's witness, the waitress became a Christian. But that didn't happen in this case. What did happen, however, is that the waitress said, "I'm glad to know about that. I might want to ask you some more about that sometime." As it worked out, the waitress moved to another job shortly thereafter, so the woman never learned whether the seed she planted bore fruit. But it does illustrate how simple it can be to offer to open the kingdom door for another person.

We may be understandably uncomfortable about doing this, though. We have seen some who do accept their faith authority become totalitarian in their witness. "Unless you accept Christ exactly in the manner I prescribe, you are not in the kingdom." "Unless you believe exactly as I do you are lost."

Christian authority is never certainty that our experience of Christ is the only possible one, but an assurance that Christ invited us all unto himself. The authority Christ gives is never totalitarian. We are stewards of the truth of God's love, but never keepers of all there is to know about God.

The act of opening the door to the kingdom for another person is a deeply satisfying one. Several years ago, the late Sam Shoemaker, a well-known pastor and author from Pittsburgh, wrote a poem called "I Stand By the Door." In that poem he said that he saw his role as a Christian as one who stands by the door of the kingdom of God to show people where the door is located and to encourage them to enter. Here is an excerpt from his poem:

> *The most tremendous thing in the world*
> *Is for [people] to find that door — the door to God.*
> *The most important thing any [person] can do*
> *Is to take hold of one of those blind, groping hands,*
> *And put it on the latch — the latch that only clicks*
> *And opens to the [person's] own touch.*
> *[People] die outside that door, as starving beggars die*
> *On cold nights in cruel cities in the dead of winter —*
> *Die for want of what is within their grasp.*
> *They live, on the other side of it — live*
> *because they have not found it.*
> *Nothing else matters compared to helping them find it,*
> *And open it, and walk in, and find [God]...*
> *So I stand by the door.*[51]

What all of this means for us is that we can author others into the faith. We can use our key to open the kingdom door for them. The church is still only built on the rock of faith authority. When that is missing, we become little more than a social club. Without the faithful kingdom "door opening" of our own age, the next generation will not come in. We do indeed hold the keys to the kingdom of heaven in our hands.

You and I, and others around the world who confess the lordship of Christ, are the church. It is built on the authority of faith in Christ. We have been invited into that faith. It is our privilege and responsibility to see that the church lives on, for the authority first given to the apostles at Caesarea Philippi centuries ago is in our hands today.

# Endnotes

1  The other locations where Matthew used disciple as a verb are 13:52 and 27:57; the verb usage is found elsewhere in the New Testament only in Acts 14:21.

2  "Class 1: What Is Discipling?" Capitol Hill Baptist Church, September 7, 2016, www.capitolhillbaptist.org/sermon/class-1-what-is-discipling/.

3  *The New Interpreter's Bible*, Vol VIII (Abingdon, 1995), pp. 502-503.

4  Acts 1:15.

5  Some parts of this also appeared in my book, *He Walked in Galilee* (Abingdon, 2005).

6  See also Luke 6:18-19; 13:32.

7  See, for example, Matthew 9:30-31.

8  Richard Conniff, "Families That Open Their Homes to the Sick," *Time*, December 5, 1988, 12-14.

9  "Michelle Froome brands Muslims 'a drain on modern society' in social media tirade," *Cycling Weekly*, April 15, 2024, www.cyclingweekly.com/news/michelle-froome-brands-muslims-a-drain-on-modern-society-in-social-media-tirade.

10  See, for example, "Chris Froome's wife calls Muslims 'a drain on society' in hateful Gaza rant," *Independent*, April 16, 2024, www.independent.co.uk/news/uk/home-news/chris-froome-michelle-froome-muslims-twitter-post-b2529584.html.

11  Naomi LaChance, "Study Shows People Still Love Inappropriately Referencing Nazis Online," *NPR, All Tech Considered*, May 9, 2016, www.npr.org/sections/alltech-considered/2016/05/09/477057058/study-shows-people-still-love-inappropriately-referencing-nazis-online.

12 Charles Krauthammer, "Stupid vs. Evil?" *Townhall*, July 26, 2002, https://townhall.com/columnists/charleskrauthammer/2002/07/26/stupid-vs-evil-n1045865#google_vignette.

13 Virginia Heffernan, "What can you do about the Trumpites next door?" *Los Angeles Times*, February 5, 2021, www.latimes.com/opinion/story/2021-02-05/trumpite-neighbor-unity-capitol-attack.

14 "Our Faith and Beliefs," www.christadelphia.org/belief.php.

15 Ibid.

16 *Shaliah* does not occur in the Bible as a noun, though the verb *lishloach* ("to send") is frequently used to describe sending a messenger or agent.

17 The *Didache* also has the title, *The Lord's Teaching Through the Twelve Apostles to the Nations*.

18 *Didache* 11:3-7, www.earlychristianwritings.com/text/didache-lightfoot.html.

19 Richard Wurmbrand, *Christ in the Communist Prisons*, p.18.

20 "The Missionary Doctor," *Time*, June 8, 1987, p. 22.

21 https://bringingalongocd.blogspot.com/

22 "What is OCD & Scrupulosity?" *The OCD Foundation*, https://iocdf.org/faith-ocd/what-is-ocd-scrupulosity/.

23 Rebecca Ruiz. "Why St. Ignatius Should Be Our Go-To Saint if We Are Suffering or Experiencing Unexpected Changes," *IgnatianSpirituality.com*, www.ignatianspirituality.com/why-st-ignatius-should-be-our-go-to-saint-if-we-are-suffering-or-experiencing-unexpected-changes/.

24 Jaimie Eckert, "Scrupulosity: The Ultimate Guide (Updated 2024)," *Scrupulosity Solutions*, https://scrupulosity.com/scrupulosity.

25 "Scrupulosity," *Dictionary of Pastoral Care and Counseling* (Abingdon Press, 1990), p. 1120.

26 "49 OCD Statistics: How Many People Have OCD?" *Golden Steps ABC*, January 2, 2024, www.goldenstepsaba.com/resources/ocd-statistics.

27 Frederick Buechner, *The Hungering Dark* (New York: Seabury Press, 1968), 28.

28 "Husbands who kiss their wives regularly live longer than those who don't, says study," *Times of India*, June 2, 2023, https://timesofindia.indiatimes.com/life-style/relationships/love-sex/husbands-who-kiss-their-wives-regularly-live-longer-than-those-who-dont-says-study/photostory/75248220.cms.

29 Or, depending on your acceptance of how the Gospel writers shaped the accounts about Jesus, it's possible that the parable of the weeds among the wheat was as Jesus originally told it, but that the interpretation narrative is Matthew's own composition to raise the topic of eschatological judgment. (See, for example, the commentary on Matthew 13:36-43 in *The New Interpreter's Bible*, Vol. VIII, page 310.)

30 See, for example, the entry "Parable" in *The Dictionary of Bible and Religion*, especially the last paragraph on page 775.

31 The liturgy was included in *Worship Aids for a Space Age*, by Bernard T. Lomas and George A. Parsons (Laymen's Press, Cope Inc., n.d.).

32 "Here's why road rage is on the rise," *Salon*, January 14, 2024, www.salon.com/2024/01/14/road-rage-increase/.

33 "40-Year Ban on Gay Clergy Struck Down," *UM News*, May 1, 2024, www.umnews.org/en/news/40-year-ban-on-gay-clergy-struck-down, and "Church Ends 52-Year-Old Anti-Gay Stance," *UM News*, May 2, 2024, https://www.umnews.org/en/news/church-ends-52-year-old-anti-gay-stance.

34 "'A Step Back in Time': America's Catholic Church Sees an Immense Shift Toward the Old Ways," *AP News*, May 1, 2024, https://apnews.com/article/catholic-church-shift-orthodoxy-tradition-7638fa2013a593f8cb07483ffc8ed487.

35 Ibid.

36 William Barclay, *The Gospel of Matthew*, Vol. 2, Revised Edition (Westminster Press, 1975), pp. 90-91. I updated the quote slightly to use inclusive language.

37 "Conservative pastor says he will 'live in to new reality' in the UMC," UM News, May 13, 2024, https://www.holston.org/article/randy-frye-post-gc-18362101.

38 I am indebted to Roger E. Van Harn in "Eleventh Sunday After Pentecost, Year A," in *The Lectionary Commentary — The Third Readings: the Gospels* (Eerdmans, 2001), pp. 82-83 for this information about the usage of *anachoreo*.

39 See, for example, Mark 1:35-39.

40 Compare today's text with Mark 6:45-52 and John 6:16-21.

41 See Matthew 8:14-15; Mark 1:29-31; Luke 4:38-39.

42 For more plot description of these two episodes of *The Chosen* containing Simon's backstory, see Kevin Keating, "The Chosen Season 3 Episode 7 and Episode 8: Recap, Review, & Analysis," *The Bible Artist*, February 3, 2023, www.thebibleartist.com/post/episode-7-episode-8-of-the-chosen-season-3-recap-review-analysis.

For a video of the walking-on-water/Eden scene, see "Jesus walks on water ... but walks with Simon." www.google.com/search?q=the+chosen+episode+where+Simon+walks+on+water&rlz#fpstate=ive&vld=cid:d4258649,vid:O7WWi65g-b14,st:0

43 J. Clinton McCann Jr., writing on the Psalms in *The New Interpreter's Bible*, Vol. IV, p; 983.

44 Ibid, p. 985.

45  Matthew 8:5-13.

46  Martin Luther, "Sermon 35," *Church Postil*, https://sermons.martinluther.us/sermon35.html)

47  ChatGPT Feb 13 (2023) Version. Free Research Preview, https://chat.openai.com/chat, accessed February 17, 2023.

48  Most of this is from my book, *He Walked in Galilee* (Abingdon, 2005).

49  J. T. Forestell, *Proclamation*, Series A, Pentecost 2 (Philadelphia: Fortress Press, 1975), 26.

50  Matthew 28:16-20. Further, Jesus speaks of Peter having authority to bind and loose, which probably meant that Peter could issue rulings about what could and could not be done by members of the Christian community. In other places, Jesus extended this binding-and-loosing authority to the whole band of apostles (See Matthew 18:18; John 20:23).

51  Quoted by Helen Smith Shoemaker in *I Stand By the Door*, (Word Books, 1967), ix.

www.ingramcontent.com/pod-product-compliance
Lightning Source LLC
Chambersburg PA
CBHW021019090426
42738CB00007B/832